BUCKEYE

DREAMS

The Tyler "Tank" Whaley Story

Go Bucks!

Tyler -42- TANK Whaley

Ken Gordon

Blue River Press
Indianapolis

LCCN Control Number: 2008931210

Cover designed by Phil Velikan.
Editorial assistance provided by Dorothy Chambers.
Book packaged by Wish Publishing.

Printed in the United States of America
10 9 8 7 6 5 4 3 2 1

Distributed in the United States by
Cardinal Publishers Group
www.cardinalpub.com

*To Dean Hume, who 25 years ago helped me discover a gift;
and to my beloved grandmother, Ruth Gordon, 1919-2008.*

Table of Contents

Foreword

by Mark Snyder

Mark Snyder is the head football coach at Marshall University. An Ironton native, he was an Ohio State defensive assistant coach from 2001 through 2004.

As football coaches, we often get caught up in a numbers game. We always want the biggest and strongest players possible. We want kids who look the part.

However, every so often a young man comes around and defies the stereotypes. He may not be highly rated by the recruiting web sites. His measurables may not attract scouts from every school in the country. His high school film may not knock everyone's socks off.

But when it comes down to it, one quality can trump all others: heart.

That is one of Tyler Whaley's strongest qualities. What he lacks in size, he makes up for in passion for the game.

His passion for the game is what allowed him to get on the field in a national championship game. That same passion and determination earned him the respect from everyone involved at Ohio State, one of the best programs in the history of college football.

During Tyler's time at OSU, he proved to be a rugged, hardnosed player with a never-say-quit, never-back-down attitude.

He was always up for the challenges and obstacles he faced. His passion for the game on the field and in the weight room was incredibly contagious.

He had unique and special leadership qualities about him that rubbed off on players, coaches and others around him. Those qualities are so rare, especially when it comes to walk-ons.

Tyler's leadership skills and selfless attitude are what eventually earned him a scholarship, but those same qualities allowed him to earn the respect of his coaches and peers long before his scholarship was awarded.

Over the course of his career at Ohio State, Tyler served as a backup to current NFL center Nick Mangold, and while playing on the scout team he went up against a wealth of NFL talent that includes A.J. Hawk, Darrion Scott, Will Smith, Bobby Carpenter, Simon Fraser, Quinn Pitcock, Tim Anderson and Anthony Schlegel.

Tyler always managed to hold his own against some of the most talented defensive players in the Ohio State program. Week in and week out, his attitude and hard-nosed physical play adequately prepared our defensive unit for our opponents. He truly made us a better unit.

I had the pleasure of recruiting Tyler out of my alma mater, Ironton High School in Ironton, Ohio. Ironton is a small town on the Ohio River of a little over 11,000 people, once known for its abundance of iron ore. Ironton High School is well known for its rich football tradition in southern Ohio.

Tiger Football is a staple in the town, and it is not uncommon to see more than the town's population at a high school football game on a Friday night in the fall.

Tyler brought a solid work ethic with him to Ohio State, which was a direct product of his growing up in Ironton.

Tyler's strong family background served as the base for his determination and never-back-down mentality. As I got to know his family, I gained a sense of how important they were to him.

He took being part of The Ohio State University football family seriously, and it echoed on the field, in the classroom, and in his social life. He always took pride in who he was and whom he represented.

Each Saturday he buckled his shoulder pads, laced his pants, and put on his silver helmet and was proud to wear it. He did not take what he had for granted like so many; he wore his uniform and ran out of the tunnel with a certain amount of humility and pride.

Now, five years later, I could not be more proud of the man that Tyler grew up to be. He always strived for excellence and never backed down from any challenges.

Tyler is a phenomenal example of a young man who was given an opportunity of which he took full advantage. He overcame a tremendous amount of adversity to defy stereotypes and exceed expectations.

Prologue

Victory over Michigan was imminent when the enormity of his achievement finally hit Ohio State fullback Tyler "Tank" Whaley.

He was standing behind and to the right of quarterback Todd Boeckman. At the end of a cold wet day in Michigan Stadium, the Buckeyes were ahead 14-3 and bunched up tightly, ready to kneel down on the final snap.

This was the play all Ohio State players dream of participating in. Since OSU was at the Michigan 5-yard line, taking a knee would be an act of mercy – they could probably score again, but they won't. How patronizingly sweet.

Whaley's job was simply to watch and make sure Boeckman touched his knee to the turf with the ball still in hand.

When that simple feat was done, Whaley threw his stocky arms in the air, turning toward fans and friends on the OSU sideline, looking to share his glee.

As celebrations go, it wasn't particularly noteworthy. Chad Johnson, "Ocho Cinco" of Cincinnati Bengals fame, would be ashamed.

Whaley, though, had overcome so much just to be on the field for that play. He had spent years as a lowly walk-on, trained to be seen and not heard, never drawing attention to himself.

So this simple gesture – his upraised arms – was his way of releasing five years of physical and emotional struggle.

It symbolized his triumph over naysayers who told him a 5-foot-11 offensive lineman would never play for the Buckeyes. He paid his own way for three years and was treated as a second-class citizen and a blocking dummy for countless hours of practice, with no immediate hope of seeing the field.

His joy came in realizing he had lived the dream that so many

Ohio kids have, of pulling on that Buckeyes jersey, running out of the Ohio Stadium tunnel, and in the end, actually playing and contributing his own small piece to the program's storied tradition.

Tyler Whaley's story sounds too good to be true: a tale of determination, hard work, perseverance, of pulling himself up from the bottom and realizing his ultimate dream? Please. In this age of BALCO and Spygate, where we learn not to trust winners (see Marion Jones, Bill Belichick, Roger Clemens, Floyd Landis, and so on), is this Whaley kid for real?

He is, and part of what makes his story compelling is that he is Everyman. He could be any one of us. He's the kind of guy who could walk through a crowded mall, and nobody's head would turn, wondering if he was some famous football player they should recognize. He looks more like someone who would come fix your hot-water heater.

He's not 6-5 or 320 pounds. He can't run a 4.4-second 40. He's not sculpted. In fact, he's got a gut, no getting around it – one that evendrew attention on national television last year.

At least twice in his life, the folks at tuxedo-rental shops have called to double-check that his measurements were correct. A size 50 jacket with a 30-inch inseam for the pants? For real?

He grew up in Ironton, a small town in southern Ohio that has been hit hard by plant closings in recent decades.

Whaley was a fine baseball and football player in high school, but nobody thought his athletic career would go any further. That 5-11 thing stopped recruiters in their tracks.

"A lot of people said, 'No, you can't do it,'" Whaley said. "Everybody said, 'He's too little or too slow.' It was always fuel for the fire, kind of, thinking back to things like that."

At this point, you may be thinking this is another "Rudy" story, an Ohio State version of the 1993 movie about Notre Dame walk-on Daniel "Rudy" Ruettiger. Both were from small towns, and both lived out a dream by joining a football program with rich tradition.

Tammy Vogelsong, Tyler's mother, said so many people started comparing the two that she finally rented the movie recently. She found herself in tears, marveling at some of the similarities.

But though the stories start the same, they end much differently.

"It's beyond Rudy," said Andy Whaley, one of Tyler's uncles. "Way beyond Rudy."

Rudy saw the field only for the last two plays of the last game of his collegiate career, and then only because his teammates demanded it.

This is nothing against Rudy, but in a way, he was a glorified mascot.

The key difference in their stories is that Tyler Whaley earned a scholarship and playing time, first a little and then, in 2007, a lot. His was not a token appearance. What he got was not out of sympathy, but because he was good enough, plain and simple.

He's called "Tank" in part because of his body build, and he has no problem poking fun at himself. He's a fun-loving, story-telling, belly-laughing kind of guy, someone whose default mode is goofy.

The man met his fiancée at a 1980s-themed party by serenading her with a heavy-metal air-guitar performance.

He's truly a good guy, one of those people who likes everyone and whom everyone likes. When you sit and talk with him, he's interested in you and what you have to say, which is not the case with many athletes accustomed to being the center of attention.

There's genuine warmth in his words and his smile.

At the same time, though, this soft exterior hides a steely core. Physically and mentally, he's a Mack truck, a ball of wound-up bulldog determination.

None of those college recruiters could see or measure his inner drive. He believes strongly in himself.

"I kept thinking, 'They have no idea what he's capable of,'" Vogelsong said of the recruiting process that passed Tyler by. "You have to know what a person has inside."

Tyler doesn't talk about himself much, doesn't brag or draw attention. But he has almost scary single-mindedness of purpose, one that paid off with success that no one predicted.

"When Tyler tells me, 'I can do this,' that's it, in my mind," said Tommy Tipton, his grandfather. "He knows what he wants to do, and he does it. That's the way he's been with everything he's done."

His mother said one of Tyler's coaches once told her that if he told Tyler to run through a brick wall, he'd go through a brick wall.

"Don't tell him that, then," she replied.

"He thinks he can do anything," she said. "If he thought he could take that big body and fly off a cliff, he'd probably try it."

Knowing as much as I do about him now, it's embarrassing to admit that even though I cover Ohio State for the *Columbus* (Ohio) *Dispatch*, Whaley was on the roster for three years before I met him or could even have picked him out of a lineup.

I first interviewed him just prior to the 2006 season, when Whaley was one of several walk-ons to be awarded scholarships. I remember being struck by how truly grateful and excited he was. His attitude was refreshing.

Even though he played in some big games that season, I didn't interview him again until midway through the 2007 campaign. That's when he came to the interview room and began to spill his life story. It was great stuff.

Afterward, I pulled him aside and said I'd like to do a feature on him during the slow period between the Michigan game and the bowl game. He was enthusiastic about it.

That's how I ended up in Ironton last December, and when I realized his story was too big to be contained on a newspaper page. I met his family, warm and loving people with fascinating stories to tell. I got a bellyful of steak and salad, as well as Dotty Tipton's hash-brown casserole, which could win awards.

I got a tour of town, during which I sensed the pride folks there had that Tyler had made it to the big-time. Ironton hasn't had enough success stories lately.

Overwhelmed, as we parted ways that evening I said to him, "Man, you could be a book."

And so it is.

Whaley, though, doesn't need public validation to feel successful. He was OK with making it onto the Buckeyes' roster, even as a lowly walk-on.

He believed he could play, but he already had proved something to himself and others just by being allowed to call himself a Buckeye, practice with the star players, dress for games and stand on the sidelines.

He'd already beat the odds just by making it that far.

But year by year, his story kept getting better. First he got the scholarship. Then he rose to second string.

And then came 2007, the year everything came together. He was moved from center to fullback, which maybe was where he should have been all along.

Also by then, the team dynamic had changed dramatically.

In 2006, the Buckeyes were a constellation of stars, led by Heisman Trophy quarterback Troy Smith and receiver Ted Ginn Jr. The team started the year ranked No. 1 in all the polls and stayed on top until that final, disastrous national championship game.

With Smith and Ginn gone last season, though, Whaley's senior class consisted mostly of walk-ons like himself. Even many of the better players were not highly touted recruits. Many had a blue-collar, humble work ethic, such as quarterback Todd Boeckman and linebacker James Laurinaitis.

In this atmosphere, Whaley fit in perfectly. The expectations were low for Ohio State, just as they were for him when he arrived at OSU. Just as he used doubters as motivation, so too did the Buckeyes as a team.

"A lot of (his teammates) went through what I went through," Whaley says, "and I know what kind of person that made me."

That's how the Buckeyes ended up celebrating on the cold, wet Michigan Stadium turf last fall, basking in a third straight Big Ten championship and a fourth straight win over their archrivals.

Whaley can't explain exactly where his doggedness comes from. He's always had it, he shrugs.

But it didn't form in a vacuum. He is a product of his surroundings. His hometown is full of tough people, people who keep picking themselves up and moving forward after disasters both natural and economic.

It's fitting, then, that these people love their football. They once were home to a team that beat the best the NFL had to offer. They built that team a stadium, a place townspeople still pack to the rafters to watch their beloved high school club play.

His own family is typical hardy Ohio River-town stock. The Whaleys and Tiptons have survived wars, layoffs and closings, and numerous health scares. And yet, like Tyler, they carry on with humor and without complaint, supporting and loving each other always.

So to begin to understand how Whaley rose from nothing to something, you have to start where I did, in his hometown.

You have to know that Tyler Whaley gets his iron from Ironton.

CHAPTER 1:
Furnaces and Football

From its very beginning, the people of Ironton were not only unafraid of hard work, they were actually drawn to it. They chose it. It's what the town was founded on, and what those who live there today take for granted: You put your nose down, don't complain, and do the job.

In future centuries, this would be manifested on the football field, where townspeople would flock to watch their young men grunt and strain and slam into each other.

Their stadium, all lit up in the shadow of the surrounding ridges, would roar with the yells of thousands.

But long before Ironton rocked, it was all about rocks.

The first one of note in the area's history was called "Hanging Rock." Were it located in the old West, "Hanging Rock" might have a sinister connotation, a place where outlaws met their Maker, perhaps.

But in the no-nonsense Midwest, people call it as they see it. So Hanging Rock, Ohio, was named because it's a rock outcropping that hangs over the Ohio River several hundred feet below.

It also is the site of the first settlement in Lawrence County, the southernmost county in Ohio.

Folks were drawn there because of the presence of a layer of rock not far beneath the surface: iron ore. It was reddish in appearance, but the early 19th-century pioneers saw green. There was money to be made in these hills.

The process of extracting iron involved superheating the ore – or smelting – and required construction of a furnace. The first furnace in Lawrence County was Union Furnace, built in 1826 just a few miles northwest of present-day Ironton.

Others soon followed. At least a dozen more were constructed in the county over the next 30 years. Some of them were given glorious names, such as the pair named after Italian volcanoes: Vesuvius and Etna.

The whole process was laborious. The heavy ore was mined and hauled to the furnace sites on wagons pulled over the hilly roads by oxen.

This was a brutally tough task. It doesn't take too much imagination to understand that the descendents of the men who did this eventually turned into offensive linemen.

Vast amounts of charcoal were needed to keep the furnace fires going, and that involved the cutting and burning of timber. Fortunately the Ohio woods at that time remained virtually unbroken. An early settler remarked that a squirrel could travel from Cleveland to Cincinnati without touching the ground. It provided plenty of fuel.

Company towns sprung up all over, each one presided over by whoever funded the furnace, called the "iron master."

Some of the smelted iron was made directly into the many necessary implements of frontier life: cookstoves, pots, utensils, nails and the like. But the big money came in the production of iron bars that were then shipped elsewhere for remanufacture.

To make the bars, the molten iron was directed into molds – one long trench and smaller bar-shaped molds jutting from it.

The majority of men who worked in this business either had been farmers, or at least kept farm animals at their homes. They thought the molds looked like a mother sow lying on her side with a row of piglets feeding. They called the bars "pig iron."

One handy feature of these bars was they stacked well, making them ideal to load onto boats and barges plying the nearby Ohio River.

As the industry grew, and smoke from the charcoal fires and furnaces hung over the region night and day, the iron masters realized they had a problem. The little town of Hanging Rock was located on a narrow strip of land just beneath the cliffs. It was ill-suited to accommodate the growing fleet of boats coming and going.

They commissioned a survey and found a site just a few miles upstream where the land sloped gently into the river, allowing much more space to load and unload.

In 1848, John Campbell and 24 men of the Ohio Iron and Coal Company laid out the streets of Ironton.

That was just the first collaboration of the iron masters. Their next may have been equally important. Deciding they needed a better way to transport the ore, timber and pig iron, they built a narrow-gauge railroad through the hills.

Eventually this spur became part of the DT & I Railroad. That would be the Detroit, Toledo and Ironton. Today it sounds strange to include little Ironton alongside two metropolitan cities, but that illustrates how important the town was at the time.

Ironton boomed. In the mid-19th century, nearly 70 furnaces were working in the Hanging Rock Iron Region, making it one of the world's largest iron producers. At the end of the 1850s, Ohio had more miles of railroad track than any state and ranked fourth in the nation in the value of its industrial products.

The Civil War was, of course, great for business. Iron from Lawrence County's Hecla Furnace was reportedly used to make the "Swamp Angel," a massive cannon that participated in the shelling of Charleston, South Carolina, during an 1863 campaign. From Jackson County, just north of Lawrence, came the raw material used in the *Monitor*, which defeated the Confederacy's *Merrimack* in the first battle of ironclads.

Hecla Furnace, one of the most famous of the dozens of pig-iron furnaces that dotted the landscape around Ironton from the 1820s until the early 20th century. (Photo courtesy of Lawrence County Historical Society)

The iron masters, loaded with cash, built huge Victorian-era mansions in Ironton and in the surrounding areas. Many of them survive today, and the local historical society promotes a self-guided walking tour of the old homes.

Now that they were landed gentry, the iron masters also began to show a softer side. They designated prime corner lots in downtown Ironton as sites for churches.

Many of the iron masters were of New England Presbyterian background and were staunch abolitionists. Ironton became a center for Underground Railroad activity, the entry point to freedom for many runaways crossing the river from the slave states of Virginia and Kentucky.

The town's founder, John Campbell, hid runaways in his home. Fugitives also were hidden in the iron carts, which were equipped with false bottoms and would take ex-slaves from town to the furnaces in the hills, where they could slip away into the woods for points north.

That heritage was passed on. To this day, Ironton residents say racism and prejudice are rare in town.

That's in contrast to some other areas of southern Ohio. I interviewed former Ohio State assistant coach Rudy Hubbard a few years ago. He had become OSU's first African-American assistant coach in 1968, and he spoke of the discrimination he encountered when recruiting the area in the late 1960s and early 1970s. He recalled not being able to find a motel willing to give him a room.

But Ironton developed differently. Tyler Whaley's grandfather, Tommy Tipton, remembers crossing the Ohio River to Ashland, Kentucky, when he was growing up in the 1940s and 1950s, and seeing the "colored" and "whites only" signs on the train station restrooms and waiting rooms.

"As a young person, that was shocking to you," Tipton said. "We weren't raised that way, and we wondered why they were doing that."

Connected by water and rail to major manufacturing centers, Ironton's job base eventually diversified. There were mills and factories of all kinds, and the coal industry took off with the discovery of vast deposits up and down the western Appalachian ridges of Kentucky, Ohio and West Virginia. By 1890, the town's population was nearly 11,000. There were four newspapers and 16 churches on those corner lots.

Eventually, though, the pig-iron furnaces shut down. Richer veins of iron had been discovered in the Lake Superior region. The hills also were becoming stripped bare of timber, since each furnace annually consumed roughly 300 acres of forest.

The last furnace was "blown out" around 1916. The crumbling remains of chimneys still dot the landscape of southern Ohio, tucked away and mostly overgrown. Several are now preserved on state park land such as the base of the chimney at Lake Vesuvius Recreational Area north of Ironton.

Several years ago, my family was hiking in the southern Ohio hills when we suddenly stumbled across a decrepit iron gate surrounding a few tombstones nearly lost in the undergrowth. A nearby historical marker said we were standing on the site of an old furnace town, once the bustling home of a thousand people or more. Looking around at the canopy of mature second-growth forest and shaded woodland, I mentally tipped my cap to the sweat equity that people had paid for something now almost completely swallowed back up by the land.

Ironton, then, has a history of prosperity, tied closely to the values of social conscience, hard work and pride – lots of pride. It never viewed itself as a small town, but as a vital center of commerce.

"Whatever they do, people from Ironton want to be the best," said Whaley's mother, Tammy Vogelsong.

Natives, by the way, pronounce the town name as "Arnt'n," blended together almost like a contraction. People there speak in a soft Appalachian accent, slightly lyrical, as opposed to a true drawl.

At its peak, Ironton was self-sufficient. It exported, not imported. Everything people needed was made nearby.

But as the iron ore petered out, Ironton started experiencing something of an identity crisis. There were still plenty of jobs and money in town. Compared to other nearby communities, though, Ironton was the slowest growing.

Part of that was due to geography. The town quickly expanded to the edge of the first range of hills behind the river – maybe seven to 10 blocks deep – but that was as far as it could grow. The ridges were steep.

So it was that in 1920, Ironton numbered about 14,000 people, but despite the regional and national prosperity of the decade – the Roaring 20s – it grew only to about 17,000 by 1930.

An early 20th-century view of the Ironton-Russell Bridge across the Ohio River. (Photo courtesy of Lawrence County Historical Society)

Meanwhile, in the same time period, Ashland developed a booming oil industry, doubling in size from 14,000 to 29,000. Huntington, West Virginia, about 20 miles upstream, exploded from 50,000 to 75,000 people, and Portsmouth, Ohio, from 33,000 to 42,000.

Once the center of the tri-state world, Ironton now was a little sibling. Civic leaders responded with a spate of building, as if creating steel-and-stone monuments to itself would make them feel more important.

Most of the city's best-known landmarks were built in this period, including The Marting Hotel, the Ironton-Russell Bridge (connecting to the Kentucky town of Russell), the First National Bank building and Ironton High School.

At the same time, the game of football was spreading rapidly. In its infancy, football flourished as a collection of "company teams" featuring rough-hewn men from the mills, foundries and factories of western Pennsylvania and Ohio.

It should be no surprise, then, that Ironton saw part of its soul in this gritty pastime. Hard work and brute strength were rewarded.

In 1919, a group of former Ironton High School players met to merge several existing club teams and form a new organization. Some of them had just returned from World War I and had witnessed the debut of the tank. The powerful new machine seemed an appropriate symbol for an industrial town. Thus they were dubbed the Tanks.

Immediately this new team became something the community could rally around. Ironton may have been a small city, but with a football team, it could compete with Philadelphia or Chicago or New York.

That's how the owners viewed it, anyway, and they prevailed upon local newspapers to promote it as such. To read the published accounts of the Tanks' news in those days is hilarious to sportswriters like myself, who grew up trained to maintain a strict objectivity. The stories are full of naked boosterism, promoting the epic struggle of their virtuous Tanks against villains from Athens, Portsmouth or Jackson, who were constantly accused of hiring "ringers" or otherwise trying to cheat the noble Tankmen.

Some people mistakenly refer to these early small-town clubs as semiprofessional. The Tanks originally were little more than amateurs, but over time, the team morphed to fully professional. By the time they disbanded, the Tanks boasted some of the nation's top talent, who were earning salaries comparable to or higher than what the NFL paid.

The NFL was founded in 1920, and its players had to hold full-time jobs, as well, to pay the bills. All the way up through the 1960s, it wasn't uncommon for pro players to have outside careers. The Tanks of the late 1920s, therefore, were as professional as anyone else.

The league – or "The League," as it's now known by college players – played in plenty of relatively small towns in its early years. Places like Hammond and Muncie, Indiana; Decatur, Illinois, Kenosha, Wisconsin, and Pottsville, Pennsylvania, had NFL franchises in the 1920s.

Had Ironton been an NFL club, it would not have been the smallest city to host one, not by a long shot. That honor belonged to the Oorang Indians, which in 1922 and 1923 were sponsored by the Oorang dog kennels in LaRue, Ohio (population: 800). The Indians were an all-Native American team for which an aging Jim Thorpe was player-coach.

They mercifully played only one home game in their two years of existence, and that was in the relative metropolis of Marion, 15 miles away.

Right from the start, the Tanks were popular, attracting crowds of 1,500 or more to their home in Beechwood Park. Paying crowds, that is. The team's owners were dismayed that hundreds of fans watched the games by climbing nearby trees and houses, maybe in protest that they were being charged to attend in a park that otherwise hosted events that were free to the public.

In 1924, the Tanks took on the NFL's Louisville Brecks and beat them, 41-0.

At first, the Tanks were comprised almost solely of local boys, who had year-round gainful employment in town and earned a few dollars for playing football.

Flushed with success, though, the team's management then wanted eagerly to compete with the best the nation could offer.

Think of it in modern terms like a very good Division III college team that suddenly saw a chance to jump to Division I-A. What would it do? Prevail upon the public for money to build a stadium, then go out and recruit top talent. So that's what Ironton did.

The stadium went up in a hurry, in a matter of months in 1926, and like those other aforementioned projects of the 1920s, it was paid for completely with private money. The construction cost was $33,500. It remains a point of pride in Ironton to this day that the project didn't rely on grants, loans or government assistance.

The Ironton High School football team, shown here in a 2007 game against Olentangy Liberty, still plays in Tanks Memorial Stadium. The stadium was built in 1926 and was where the Ironton Tanks played until they disbanded after the 1930 season. (Photo by Jim Ridgeway)

It was called Beechwood Stadium then. Now it's Tanks Memorial Stadium. It is unique and thoroughly charming. With its distinctive overhang roof and brick construction, it looks like a cross between Wrigley Field and the horse track at your local county fairgrounds.

The first game played there was on October 17, 1926, when a crowd of about 3,000 watched the Tanks destroy the Cleveland Indians, 47-0. That wasn't surprising, considering that at the end of the 1926 season, the Tanks were 62-5-9 in their eight-year history.

In 1927, Thorpe played a game in Ironton. The legend had been lured to serve as a player-coach for the Shoe-Steels, a team in Portsmouth, which had become Ironton's archrival.

Girded for the big time, with their new stadium, the Tanks now started to cast a wide net for talent. Team manager Nick McMahon, using the 1927 All-American list as his guide, sent letters to colleges all across the country.

He heard back from few, but one of those responses was postmarked Nebraska, where tailback Glenn Presnell expressed interest. The NFL's New York Giants also were offering him a job, paying up to $175 a game. But Ironton held an ace in this game. Presnell wanted to go into education as a career, so the Tanks outbid the Giants by offering him a $1,600-a-year teaching job at Ironton High in addition to $150 a game.

With Presnell as player-coach, the Tanks were 7-1-3 in 1928, but they slumped to 5-6 in 1929, their first losing record.

Also that year, the stock market crashed, plunging the nation into economic chaos. The Tanks suddenly were in debt, paying a steep price for their improved roster. And they didn't have the fan base of a major metropolitan area to keep the cash coming in.

Believing in the time-honored notion that fans will flock to a winning team, it was decided that in 1930, the Tanks would make bold, maybe desperate moves to improve. First they landed some first-line collegians from Michigan and Iowa.

Then they hired 39-year-old Earle "Greasy" Neale as coach, which would allow Presnell to focus on playing. Neale was accomplished, having coached the Washington & Jefferson College team to the 1922 Rose Bowl (where it fought California to a 0-0 tie).

McMahon arranged an ambitious schedule, which included three NFL teams – the Portsmouth Spartans had just joined the NFL, plus the Tanks would meet the New York Giants and Chicago Bears, both of the latter games set for Redland Field (later renamed Crosley Field) in Cincinnati.

The Tanks avenged a season-opening 7-6 loss to the Spartans with a dramatic 16-15 victory in Portsmouth. In front of a crowd of at least 7,500, Neale suited up for the first time in 12 years, caught a crucial pass, and played well on defense to help secure the win.

By this time, though, the ripple effects of the Depression were being keenly felt. McMahon first harangued the Ironton faithful to come out in large numbers. When that failed, he took the team on a barnstorming tour of sorts, looking for larger gate receipts on the road.

One of those games was in Memphis, Tennessee, the Tanks' longest-ever road trip. It wasn't a particularly noteworthy game – Ironton lost, 7-0 – except for the treatment the northern visitors received at the hands of the southern press corps.

Reading accounts of the game might remind Ohio State fans of the recent Big Ten vs. Southeastern Conference arguments that have raged the past two years. Buckeyes fans gnash their teeth at the SEC's assumed superiority, screaming and howling at the southern arrogance.

It wasn't all that different 78 years ago, apparently. Reacting to the Tanks' tough defense against backs Tony Holm and Bill Banker, the *Commercial-Appeal* writer noted, "It was rather curious to see this unheralded team from the Midwest stop the thrusts of two of the best backs the South has produced."

Another reporter for the *Press-Scimitar* kept referring to "the stubborn Oronton team."

The Tanks' crowning achievement came in November 1930, when they defeated the Giants and Bears in a two-week span.

On November 11, Presnell threw a scoring pass as time expired, for a 13-12 win over the Giants and their standout quarterback, Michigan product Bennie Friedman. Reporters noted that Presnell outplayed Friedman.

On November 23, the Tanks vanquished the Bears, 26-13, who boasted the likes of Harold "Red" Grange and Bronko Nagurski. Presnell had two TD runs, including one of 88 yards.

Irontonians rightfully still boast of these achievements. Some take exception to the fact that historians call the games "exhibition." They argue they should be referred to merely as "non-league."

They have a point, in that the Tanks were as professional as any other team operating in that day. But the media guides of the Bears and Giants today do not list those games in their accounting of the 1930 season. Since they were not officially counted, one has to consider them as exhibitions, however meaningful they were to Ironton.

Those games proved to be a final leap of flame before the Tanks burned out, deeply in debt. Though no official announcement was made for months, an era had ended.

Neale accepted the head coaching job at West Virginia University. Presnell jumped to the NFL's Spartans in nearby Portsmouth. Three years later, in 1934, the Spartans were purchased by a Detroit businessman for $7,952.08 and renamed the Lions.

Legend has it that Presnell was the one to choose the Lion's distinctive colors: Honolulu blue and silver. In 1934, he kicked a 54-yard field goal, an NFL record that held up for 19 years. In 1935, the Lions won the NFL title.

Presnell retired after the 1936 season. He coached at Nebraska, served in World War II, and later coached and was athletic director at Eastern Kentucky University until his retirement in 1974.

Married to an Ironton woman, Presnell lived the rest of his days there as a beloved figure, a symbol of the mighty Tanks. The town held several Tanks reunions, renamed the stadium Tanks Memorial Stadium, and put old team photos on the stadium's outside wall.

Presnell died in 2004 at age 99, one of the last surviving Tankmen.

If the Tanks' demise was a disappointment, it was followed by disaster. Already struggling through the Depression, Ironton was devastated by an Ohio River flood in 1937 that covered 90 percent of the town with water.

"You would think with the flood and the Depression, that it would wipe everybody out, and they would say, 'What's the use?' and give up," said Virginia Bryant, a town historian who lived through the flood as a young girl.

But that didn't happen. Bryant's family was one of many that simply moved to the upper floor of their house until the waters receded. Others pitched tents in the nearby hills and waited.

When the water went down, "my mother and others just got their brooms and swept the mud out, hosed it down, and went back to work. All of us kids went back to school."

A new floodwall went up soon afterward. Today a mural commemorating the Tanks decorates a stretch of that wall. Leather-helmeted heroes blast through would-be tacklers at the goal line, the stadium and its unique overhang visible in the background.

World War II sparked another economic revival. New industry moved in during the war and afterward. Chemical plants were paramount: Allied Chemical had three facilities in the area; Dow opened in Hanging Rock. Two cement plants opened.

Iron and steel still provided, only now they were blast furnaces and coke plants like Ironton Iron (later called Dayton Malleable). Armco Steel boomed across the river in Ashland.

Like much of the nation in the 1950s, times were good in Ironton. The downtown thrived, with most businesses locally owned.

Tommy Tipton, Tyler Whaley's grandfather, remembered the town of his boyhood as a robust city.

"My recollection was I could stand on the sidewalk and look toward the downtown area, and people were shoulder to shoulder every day, especially weekends," he said.

More hard times lay ahead, this one a slump that would drag on longer than the previous downturns.

But like Virginia Bryant's mother, the people of Ironton are tough and uncomplaining. They are descendants of the pioneers who had hauled iron ore and timber over the tortuous hills in wagons, after all.

"It's a town that's kind of run-down, but the people's spirits are high," Whaley says. "There are a lot of blue-collar, hard-working people in Ironton that deserve a lot better than they're getting. The town is still alive because of people like that."

Football remains a big part of the community's psyche. And the story of the Tanks helps explain why Ironton produced a player like Tyler Whaley, who refused to accept limits others wanted to put on him.

It's the same town, after all, whose heroes weren't afraid of Bears and Giants.

CHAPTER 2:

A Tough, Loving Lot

H is name was Alva, but his nickname was "Spike," which probably led to a few chuckles from folks at first, seeing that he stood 5-foot-3.

But like the boy named Sue of Johnny Cash fame, Spike Tipton had gravel in his guts and spit in his eye. In the early part of the 20th century, he and his wife, Carrie, raised four boys on a farm outside Ironton.

Spike also was a teamster – not in the modern sense of the word, which brings to mind truck drivers – but in the early 19th-century sense, which involved teams of mules.

Among other duties, Spike and his mule team painstakingly hauled cement up and down the hills to help construct the reservoir that would supply Ironton with water.

Spike was Tyler Whaley's great-great-grandfather, the most distant ancestor of which any of his immediate family members have memories. Spike, then, is the beginning of the common thread that binds Whaley's kind together – undersized, but tough as a two-dollar steak.

Farming was hardscrabble in the rocky hillsides of southern Ohio, and all four of Spike's boys went to work at a young age – Burdine (nicknamed "Tip"), Tom, Julius ("Jude") and Wilbur ("Webb").

Tom and Webb were close. They shared a love of hunting and apparently, carousing. Details are vague, but the phrase "fun loving" comes up a lot.

Several of the boys were working in bakeries when they grew tired of working for others and decided to open their own. Tipton Bros. Bakery, Inc., opened its doors for the first time on April Fools' Day, 1935.

It would become an Ironton institution and the family's focal point.

Tom married Opal Louise, "a little bitty woman," says her son, Tommy. "Barely 5-foot tall, but she was a little feisty thing. Everybody loved her. Even today, when people see me, they talk about her."

Opal was a talker and an entertainer, Tommy said. "She had a million stories to tell. She'd talk your leg off."

She counts as the second of Tyler Whaley's small, spunky ancestors.

In 1942, Tom was drafted while Opal was pregnant. Tommy was born while his father was on a train heading to Fort Bragg. Father and son would not meet for several years.

Sent to the Pacific, Tom served in a tank destroyer unit. Toward war's end, he was one of the lucky tankers to crew the powerful new M-36. With their 90mm armament, the M-36 was nicknamed "The Slugger."

Webb, meanwhile, was killed in action during the Normandy invasion.

Whether because of the death of his brother or his own experiences in combat, or both, Tom came home a changed man. No longer was he the good-natured life of the party.

Instead he was quiet and reserved, almost to the point of being withdrawn. He threw himself into his work. Tommy recalls taking just one vacation in his childhood, and his father was miserable the entire time.

Tom also had survived a serious bout with malaria while overseas. Tommy would be their only child.

Tom was stubborn and set in his ways, but he also was a man of honor and dignity.

"Something he instilled in all of us was that you didn't have to have a paper signed if you had a handshake on it," Tommy said. "Your word was your bond."

Tommy believes his father today would have been diagnosed with post-traumatic stress disorder. Sixty years ago, though, it might have been called "combat fatigue." George Patton would have slapped a soldier for it. You didn't get therapy or antidepressants. You just dealt with it inside your own head as best you could.

Tipton's Bakery was an Ironton institution for nearly 70 years. It was founded by Tom Tipton, Tyler Whaley's great-grandfather, along with Tom's three brothers. Pictured working in the bakery are Tyler's grandfather Tommy Tipton (left), Tyler's great-uncle Julius Tipton (middle) and Tom Tipton (right). (Family photo)

Dotty Krum grew up in Coryville, just over the first hill north of Ironton. Her father, Lester, was a lifer at Ironton Iron. She graduated from Rock Hill High School in 1959 and took a job at the Tipton bakery.

The Tipton brothers had bought a building down the street and opened up a grocery store, but the bakery remained the heart of the operation.

A year behind Dotty in school, Tommy Tipton immediately set his sights on her, telling friends that's who he would marry. He was right. They were married in 1961.

"I told Tommy he just saw me as a good investment," Dotty says, good-naturedly. "He knew I was a good employee and he wanted to keep me working the rest of my life."

The new couple quickly had two daughters, Tammy and Kim. Eight years after Kim, Dotty was pregnant again when a customer came into the store and asked when she was due.

April, came Dotty's answer. Oh how sweet, the woman said. If it's a girl, you'll have to name her April.

Tommy, listening nearby, betrayed his preference by growling, "Have you ever heard of a boy named April?"

The baby girl was born early, in March, sparing Dotty from having to explain to her customer why she was named Missy. By the next year, with Dotty expecting her fourth, Tommy actually was rooting against having a boy, who he figured would be spoiled and ruined, anyway, by the four females in the house.

Angie Tipton's arrival completed the family in 1974.

Like his father, Tommy was a workaholic as well. He'd get up at 2 a.m. to bake, spend the morning at the bakery, then head to the store in afternoon. Still, he managed to make it to all his daughters' events, and they were an active bunch: softball, volleyball, dance recitals, band concerts.

"No matter what it was, he was there, even if he only got an hour of sleep," Missy says. "Mom and Dad were really supportive."

Tommy even found time to coach some of the girls' softball teams. The only thing he had difficulty finding was time in the bathroom.

Tammy was gifted, Tommy decided, after coming home from work one day and seeing what his 2-year-old daughter had created. It was a three-dimensional diorama constructed in a shoebox, complete with trees topped with cotton balls. She was just a baby.

She grew into a vivacious, active teen. She was an entertainer. She loved to dance, was a majorette at Ironton High School, and took part in pageants and school plays. She also took art classes, where she was so good at painting that her teacher set up classes for her at an art gallery in Huntington, West Virginia.

It came naturally. She could take one look at you and sketch your likeness, just like that. She came back from Huntington one day and created a detailed oil painting of a beach scene, though she had never been to the ocean.

Her dancing and majorette duties allowed her to travel to various summer camps and competitions. After graduation from Ironton High in 1980, Tammy headed to Dayton, where she worked for Fred Miller studios as a dance instructor.

She was feeling the pull of the exciting big world outside the familiar comforts of Ironton and home. Nobody in the family had ever left the area, at least not for long.

What happened next is interpreted differently among family members. The fact is that Tammy moved back home to Ironton. Why she moved back is where it gets fuzzy.

"Mom and Dad kind of panicked and wanted me to come home," Tammy says. "They didn't want their first-born to take off and not come back. I always wanted to go to art school and be a dancer, but my mom and dad had more concrete dreams. There was a lot more stability at home."

Tommy and Dotty don't remember it that way. They saw the Fred Miller experience more as a summer job, then Tammy came home to find permanent work.

She had two jobs, at a bank and a clothing store. When the bank job was eliminated, Tammy asked her father if she could work in the family store, specifically to use her artistic ability to decorate cakes.

Dotty had mastered the basics of decorating, but true to form, Tammy took one look at how it was done, jumped right in, and started producing amazing creations.

She quickly gained a reputation around town, with her cakes in heavy demand. It would turn into her life's work.

When Tyler tells his mother's story, it has a whiff of sadness to it. That's interesting, since he obviously had to form this opinion secondhand. His views have been shaped from snippets of conversations, or maybe just a sense of what his mother felt about how her life turned out.

To him, she is a hero, someone who made a noble sacrifice for the sake of family. Before the 2007 season, when it was his turn to make the traditional senior speech, he got up in front of his Ohio State teammates and spoke in touching and dramatic terms about his mother's life.

"She had ambitions, she didn't want to stand behind a counter and draw on cakes for a living at first," Tyler says. "But she did what she thought she had to do."

Twenty-five years later, Tammy still has that same vivacious-teen personality. She is outgoing and almost impossibly sweet. To her, the world consists of two types of people: those she knows, and those she'd like to meet.

Five minutes with her, and you're talking like old friends. If you haven't hugged yet, you're about to.

She doesn't spend much time dwelling on the past. Her life has turned out well. Her parents and three sisters all live in Ironton, within a few minutes' drive, and she's content.

"When you're 18, you want to go somewhere else," she says. "I tried to spread my wings a little bit. But I didn't want to leave Mom and Dad. Everyone I loved was back home, and I love being around my family."

No matter how she says she views her experience today, though, it had one lasting effect: When it came time for her kids to want to leave the nest, she would encourage them to fly.

"I want them to see the world," she says, "and do whatever they want to do."

Meanwhile, across town, Tom and Marie Whaley were raising eight kids. Seven of those kids came in a 10-year span, and then, after a 12-year gap, Andy Whaley, No. 8, arrived.

They were a Catholic family, but they turned their backs on Notre Dame's Golden Dome and were huge Ohio State football fans. As Tyler says, the Whaley clan is "ate up" with Buckeye football.

In the middle of that pack was Rich. He attended St. Joseph Central, Ironton's Catholic school, and played football, basketball and baseball, though he says he didn't excel in any particular sport.

He was a good enough fullback and cornerback in football, though, that after graduation in 1975, he went on to play for Otterbein College, a Division III school in Westerville, Ohio.

As he says, "Things just didn't work out for me there," and he dropped out after several years. He returned to Ironton, where he was in and out of jobs, a pattern that would continue for awhile.

Rich Whaley and Tammy Tipton met, then got married in October 1982.

On what otherwise was a joyous occasion, 10-year-old Missy Tipton – serving as a flower girl, along with her sister Angie – sobbed all the way up the aisle of the church.

For years, Tammy had let Missy sleep in her bed. Theirs was an especially tight bond.

"We were extremely close, and when she got married, I was devastated," Missy says. "It's like I lost my best friend. To me, she was moving out and would never come back."

The whole family remains tight. Missy says it's rare that a day goes by without her seeing her parents or sisters. They all talk by phone several times a day.

"I've been told many times by people, they'll come up to me and say they wish they had what we have," she says. "The world would be a better place if everybody had the love and support that we have. We're just really fortunate."

Tammy and Rich welcomed their son to the world on Sept. 15, 1984. They named him Justin Tyler Whaley, but always called him Tyler.

Rich didn't realize it at the time, but he would end up living vicariously through Tyler. Rich grew up in that big family of Buckeye fans, dreaming he might one day play at Ohio State.

But he is candid about his own shortcomings, recognizing he didn't have the heart or desire to reach that goal.

"That's why I admire Tyler," Rich says. "It takes a lot of hard work and determination and heart to make a dream come true. I always tell him I wish I had grown up to be like him."

We're skipping ahead in Tyler's life. At this point, he's a newborn.

But knowing what we know about him now, we can look back and see how he carries the echoes of all who came before: the toughness of blue-collar workers such as Spike Tipton, Lester Krum and Tom Whaley, the stubbornness of Tom Tipton, the work ethic of Tommy and Tammy Tipton, the life spirit and entertainer qualities of Opal Tipton and Tammy, and the unfulfilled hopes and dreams of his father.

And through all of it, weaving and binding tight, ran the thread of a family's love.

CHAPTER 3:
The Making of a Tank

Can a newborn really push himself up and look around? That's the question Tyler Whaley's family still debates to this day, thanks to a grandfather's story and a mysterious missing video.

Tommy Tipton first saw his grandson when Tyler was about seven hours old, barely out of the delivery room. Tommy was by himself, taping the momentous occasion in the nursery, when he says the little guy pushed his head and shoulders up off the crib sheet.

Tyler has recounted the story to friends in the years since.

"They gave me crap for that, (saying), 'There is no way a baby can do that...that's impossible,'" Tyler said. "But that's what my grandpa says."

Tyler's mother, Tammy, also doubts it. Tommy stands by his story, but so far has not been able to produce the tape to prove it.

It's better this way, a legend that lives on, the Whaley version of Babe Ruth calling his shot.

What's undeniable is that Tyler spent his formative years in a sports-crazy environment, getting it both from his town and his family.

The Tanks had been defunct for 54 years by the time Tyler was born, but Ironton had never lost its love for football. By 1984, Ironton High had been coached by Bob Lutz for 12 years and had established quite a legacy. A state title in 1979 would be followed by another in 1989, when Tyler was 4.

With his aunts active in softball, little Tyler was constantly being carted around in a stroller to the ballfields or to Tanks Memorial Stadium. He had a ball of some sort in his hands just about from the moment he could stand.

Ironton is sort of a less-famous version of Massillon, Ohio, where babies are given little footballs in the maternity wards. That's a cute publicity stunt, but can Massillon newborns lift their heads at seven hours old?

Tyler's father, Rich Whaley, meanwhile was battling intermittent employment and some personal issues, which he sums up as "carrying on irresponsibly." His and Tammy's marriage suffered and ended after just four years with dissolution in 1986.

Tyler was 2, so he doesn't remember a time when his parents were together. What he does remember, though, is how smoothly everyone handled the situation, resulting in the best possible upbringing under the circumstances.

As Tyler grew, he never heard any hard feelings or negativity expressed by either parent. Even though her extended family certainly could help her care for Tyler, Tammy made sure Rich was an important part of his son's life.

"Tammy is really a forgiving person," says Missy Leonard, Tammy's younger sister. "Richie had his faults, but she never talked bad about his father. I think that helped Tyler grow into such a good young man."

Another important person in Tyler's upbringing soon came into the picture. Dave Vogelsong was a single father in 1987 when he met Tammy Tipton. It must have felt right, because they met on July 4, and he proposed to Tammy 16 days later. They married in September.

Whitney Vogelsong, a few years older than Tyler, became his stepsister.

Dave was – and is – a steadying influence. First he provided financial stability for Tammy and Tyler. He has worked at Dow Chemical in Hanging Rock for nearly 30 years.

And at home, Dave is a perfect foil to Tammy's effusiveness. Kind, quiet and dependable, Dave is like a silent partner. It works – they will celebrate their 21st anniversary this fall.

Though Tyler lived with his mother, he spent lots of time with both sets of grandparents as well as his father. Rich's parents had those eight kids, so when Tyler went to their house – traditionally, for Sunday dinners – he had a whole pack of Whaley cousins to play with.

His uncle Andy Whaley said Tyler had a "have bag, will travel" childhood at times.

Tammy's younger sisters were 12 and 10 when Tyler was born, so they treated him more like a baby brother than a nephew.

After raising four girls, Tommy Tipton was thrilled to finally have a boy in the family. A hardcore sports fan who also had the work ethic of someone who owned his own successful business, Tommy was an important influence on young Tyler.

Tammy remembers taking Tyler along while she taught dance classes in Ironton.

"My dad would say, 'Don't encourage that,' and I'd say, 'Dad, he's fine,'" she recalls.

Tyler was grandpa's little Ironton Fighting Tiger, Tommy would say.

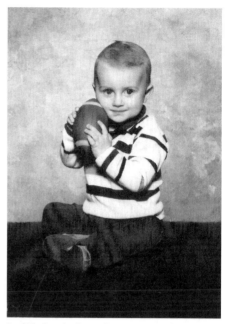

It didn't take long for young Tyler to have a football in his hands. (Family photo)

Tyler calls Tommy "my father on that side of the family, and I had my real dad, then Dave came into the picture. So I always had three dads, and they all three got along, which makes it good."

That's not just good, it's deserving of a medal of some sort. In our society, we glorify those who can run and jump, or catch and hit a ball. But where are the statues to single mothers who manage to raise well-balanced kids? Or grandparents who end up raising their grandkids unexpectedly? Or stepparents who truly love and accept stepchildren as their own?

In Tyler's case, admirable is not a strong enough word to describe all the adults who were involved in his life and who were focused on his well-being first, pushing aside their own hurts, memories and emotions.

Rich is grateful his son was surrounded by so many loved ones. Singling out Tommy and Dotty Tipton, Dave and Tammy, he says, "If anyone deserves any accolades for rearing such a wonderful person, it would be those four, especially Tammy."

He describes his ex-wife as kind, determined, hard-working and big-hearted. Then with more than a touch of self-deprecation, he adds, "That's who Tyler took after, thank God."

Growing up in Ironton, kids seem to absorb the sports culture. It just seeps through everyone's cell walls, like osmosis.

The entire town goes to the high school football games, and kids don the jersey of their favorite player. In the stands one day, Tyler declared he would be on that field when he got bigger.

He played backyard pickup games of soccer, basketball, baseball and football with that pack of Whaley cousins. It was an idyllic childhood in many ways.

"It's a small town where everybody knows everybody, and it's one of those towns where you're not afraid to let kids run around until the street lights come on," Tyler said. "It's set up good."

Many of his family members were Cincinnati pro-sports fans — Reds and Bengals — so he watched those teams on TV and did a fair imitation of the Ickey Shuffle as a 4-year-old in the fall of 1988, the season that running back Ickey Woods led the Bengals to the Super Bowl.

He didn't just watch, though. Even at a young age, he was studying the games, asking many questions and listening and thinking carefully about the answers.

But one of the earliest and most notable character traits Tyler developed was competitiveness. He couldn't handle losing at anything: card games, board games, you name it.

If things weren't going his way, the frustration would boil and he'd demand to start over, or flip the board and end the game prematurely.

Later in life, he would learn to better channel that frustration, but he held onto that desire to come out on top.

"Everything he's ever done, he tries to top somebody," Tammy says. "If a friend of his hit a home run, Tyler would try to hit one farther."

Not only that, Tammy adds, but if Tyler couldn't do something, he would practice doing it until he could. That's a rare trait for anyone, let along a young child.

Of repeating something – on his own – until he got it down, she says, "You can't make a kid do that. They've got to want it. As much as you might want it for them, you can't make them do that."

That's something innate. Tyler struggles to describe where it came from.

"I always wanted to be the best, and if I wasn't, I felt like, 'Man, I didn't do something I should've done.' That's the way I've always approached things, and I don't know how I got that."

This qualifies as another "how to parent" moment from Whaley's childhood. Rather than be pushed into sports by others, he was instead encouraged and taught. And in the end, he was propelled by his own drive. It's the best way.

But while he wonders aloud where he got that drive, it's pretty clear that it runs in his family. All those hard-working, no-non-sense Whaleys and Tiptons of past generations passed it down to him.

And the most direct line can be drawn from his mother. Tammy throws herself completely into what she is doing. She spent long hours on her feet at the bakery when Tyler was young, and he often would tag along. No doubt, her work ethic was an important influence.

"Mom works extremely hard," he says. "That's one of those things that some people have and some people may not have. She instilled me with morals and beliefs, and one that she instilled in me as a little kid was before I would start something, she would ask me, 'Do you really want to do it? Because if you start it, you're not quitting.'"

Tyler didn't stick with everything he started, though. As a little guy, he played soccer, baseball and basketball, but he eventually gave up soccer and basketball.

He played hoops just long enough for his grandfather to realize the kid had a natural athleticism.

"He was ambidextrous," Tommy Tipton says. "The first time I saw him pick up a basketball, he was dribbling with both hands and not watching (the ball)."

Basketball went by the wayside in part because Tyler was filling out, as in gaining weight. Rich attributes part of it to the fact he was always hanging around the family bakery, "and I think Tyler found out how good those donuts, pies and cakes were."

Most Ironton boys grow up hoping to play one day for the Ironton High School Tigers, and Tyler was no different. (Family photo)

Tyler loved Taco Bell as well, Rich reports. He said Tammy had Taco Bell cravings while pregnant, which might account for it.

At this point in Tyler's life, Dave was his day-to-day father. Rich would come by and pick Tyler up at times. When he and Tyler went to movies together – one of their favorite pastimes – Rich said they would buy a large popcorn with butter "and have all of it eaten before the movie started." He would have to buy another one to devour during the actual movie.

By the time he was eight, Tyler was pushing 100 pounds. That led to a disappointment when, that year, he could finally sign up to play for the Bills, an Ironton pee-wee football team.

He surpassed the weight limit to play in the backfield. This was tough to take. Like most kids, he dreamed of throwing the winning pass or running for touchdowns.

Now he'd have to learn the nuances of blocking and deal with the anonymity of playing on the line.

Again he showed some instant potential. In Tyler's first organized game at age 8, he lined up at offensive tackle. Across from him was a player about twice his size, Tommy Tipton says.

"The very first play, Tyler wasn't ready for the ball to be snapped, and the kid hit Tyler and knocked him back about four feet," Tommy says.

This is where we find out what the boy is made of, Tipton thought to himself. How will he react?

"The next play, Tyler knocked the kid back about seven feet," he said.

Heart and competitiveness had won out over sheer size. It was a prelude of things to come.

"I said, 'We're OK, we won't have to worry about this,'" Tipton said. "And that was the way he was from then on."

He had always been a huge Ohio State fan. Like so many other Ohio kids, this was mostly due to the fact that everyone else was Buckeyes crazy.

The Columbus area takes the prize for being the most nuts, of course. But after that, OSU fever seems most intense in smaller Ohio towns that aren't suburbs – places like Zanesville, Lima, Newark, Mansfield or Portsmouth, to name a few.

Growing up in Ohio, it doesn't take too long to get it in your blood. The Whaley clan, in particular, was "ate up" with Ohio State, in Tyler's words. He recalls the huge crowd at his uncle Pat Whaley's house in 1995 and 1996, when Ohio State played and beat Notre Dame in a home-and-home series.

Being Catholic, the Whaleys knew plenty of Fighting Irish fans, and they were kind enough to invite them. The carport would be divided down the middle – everyone stayed on their side.

"I just remember me and my uncles, when Ohio State scored a touchdown, getting up and doing 'Script Ohio' and playing band music," Tyler says. "Just outrageous stuff. If somebody was watching, they would have been like, 'What is going on? What is that family doing?'"

Expressing themselves, that's what. Just like Andy Whaley – Tyler's youngest uncle – had expressed his love for the Buckeyes a few years earlier.

In 1990, at age 19, Andy was just finishing up his freshman year at OSU when he was diagnosed with cancer in his chest. He underwent chemotherapy, and then surgery – laying his chest cavity open – to get the remnants that chemo had left behind.

That was in August of 1991. Doctors of course advised him to rest and take time off from school. But Andy knew that not enrolling that fall would mean not getting the football season tickets all students are allotted.

The statute of limitations hopefully has expired by now, so I'll let Andy tell the story:

"I went up and enrolled in school, then went and got the sticker on my ID that says you're a full-time student," he said. "I picked up my football tickets, and then I went right back and withdrew. But I had my tickets that fall."

Pardon the expression, but that's sick. And rest assured, the savvy ticket lords at Ohio State have long since closed that loophole.

Football would take him to Ohio State one day, but Tyler's family believed his best sport was baseball.

As with basketball and football, he showed instant ability. The first thing everyone mentions is his extraordinary hand-eye coordination. He was never going to be the fastest player, or roam centerfield, but he could hit. And with that barrel chest of his, he hit for power.

That same hand-eye ability also helped him become an outstanding defensive first baseman.

"You couldn't throw the ball by him," Tommy Tipton says. "He had the softest set of hands you've ever seen."

By the time he was 10, in the summer of 1995, Tyler was playing on an all-star traveling team. They were about to head to Dayton for the state age-group championships, when the kids decided they all needed nicknames to put on posters and display in the windows of their cars and minivans on the drive.

Tyler's neighbor and friend, Matthew White, was a natural for "Whitey," but what about Tyler?

He doesn't know whose idea it was, but "Tank" was suggested for him.

"Here's a kid that's short, stocky, powerful, so 'Tank' is perfect," he recalls. "And it kind of went with my name, Tyler 'Tank' Whaley.'"

And so it was. Tyler's team won the tournament.

The next year, 1996, Tom Tipton – Tyler's great-grandfather – lay dying of pancreatic cancer. On a visit to the hospital, Tyler brought Tom a picture he'd drawn, and he signed it "Tank."

Tom was taken aback. He told Tyler that had been his nickname in World War II, when he'd been a crew member in a tank destroyer.

Tom's son, Tommy, said that's the first the family had known of the nickname. His father had never mentioned it in the 50 years since he returned from the Pacific.

Needless to say, that revelation further cemented Tyler's nickname as "Tank."

Listening to his family tell the stories of his baseball prowess today is like sitting around a campfire and hearing about Paul Bunyan. Tank's feats have taken on an almost mythical status.

His stepfather, Dave, talks of Tank hitting balls so hard he would split aluminum bats down the middle. Good-quality youth baseball bats can run upward of $300, so the first time Tank busted one, the family requested – and received – a refund.

The next time, though, they had no such luck. The bat company refused to believe the kid had split another. Dave says Tank busted two or three. Somewhere he's got one stashed still, a souvenir of the boy's power.

Tank is a natural lefty, but batted right-handed. That's not very smart, baseball-wise, but Tommy Tipton's attitude was, "Why mess with something that works?"

That's why, when one of Tank's coaches changed his batting stance, Tommy intervened.

"The guy brought his hands in against him and dropped them down," Tommy reports. "Tank's batting average dropped and he lost his power. Now, I never interfered with his coaches, but this time I said to the guy, 'I need to talk to you. Look at (Tank's shoulders). Those hands have got to be away from him so he can get his chest through (on the swing).'"

Back in his natural stance, Tank just kept hitting.

At age 13, he was on another all-star traveling team that traveled to Dublin, Ohio, for a game against a team that looked more like a high-school squad.

"There were some boys that were 6 foot 4," Tommy says. "Tank was standing at first, and he didn't come up past the first baseman's armpits. Even when their catcher was squatting, he was taller than the umpire."

This sounds Bunyan-esque again, but it's a good story, anyway.

One of the Goliaths (we're making that up) cranked a long home run, and Tammy, Dotty and Tank's aunt Missy all started imploring Tank to match it.

Like any self-respecting kid, he looked to strike a deal. "What do I get if I hit one?" he said.

Now, Tommy must not have been in earshot, because he didn't believe in this. You don't bribe kids. They have to do something because they want to. And anyway, everyone knows if you try to hit a home run, you overswing and miss the ball.

In a weak moment, though, Dotty told Tank they would build a pool if he knocked one out. For years, Dotty's girls had bugged their parents for an inground pool.

Sure enough, "He hit one way, way out," Dotty says. "A no-doubter."

Tommy heard a commotion in the stands and turned to see the women whooping and hollering while flailing their arms in imaginary crawl strokes.

"What the heck are you doing?" he asked.

"We're swimming," they shouted. "You're getting a pool."

Tommy and Dotty did build a pool, and it quickly became a favorite postgame gathering place for Tank and his teammates.

When he wasn't playing sports, though, and maybe in spite of Tommy's best efforts, Tank also exhibited a softer side, as well as signs that he had inherited some of the entertainer genes from his dancer-artist-majorette mother.

As Vince McMahon might tell you, who puts on a better show than professional wrestling? His great-grandfather Tom Tipton was a big wrestling fan, and when Tank was just a little guy, he was hooked. He loved Hulk Hogan, so Tammy would make him "muscle suits" he could strap on and pretend to be huge. He would run around, flexing his biceps and "grrr-ing."

If he didn't get a wrestling toy on Christmas or birthdays, he was disappointed.

Not surprisingly for a natural showman, Tank thrived in the spotlight. That was evident on an old video that the family still laughs about.

Tank's half-sister Madison was born in January 1989 to Dave and Tammy. Dave was taping Madison in a baby swing one day later that year. In the background, Tank can be heard pleading, over and over, "Dave, look at me. Hey Dave, what about ME? Watch ME, Dave."

Who knows what he was doing. What got his family laughing were his constant and plaintive cries for attention.

The family says he's a very good dancer, which Tank jokes is because Tammy was teaching dance while pregnant with him. Add that to Taco Bell cravings on the list of prenatal gifts Tammy may have given her son.

In school, Tank was just as driven as he was on the ball fields. At home, he rarely got in trouble.

"He never gave us any grief at all," Dave says. "He was always wanting to please you. Some kids push their parents' buttons a little, but he would never do that. He never did anything to ruffle our feathers, he was always worrying about being a good kid."

His grandmother Dotty Tipton said she and Tommy spent so much time carting Tank around that some people thought they were his parents. Needless to say, he grew close to his grandparents.

"When he was little, if we'd leave or drop him off at home, he would always say, 'Bye Mamaw, bye Papaw, I love you,'" Dotty said. "I told Tommy once that pretty soon we won't hear that anymore, when he gets too old he won't want his friends to hear him say that."

But he never quit saying it. Even through those awkward teenage years, he never felt self-conscious.

"He always did – he didn't care if he was with friends or strangers or his girlfriend," Dotty says. "He was with his prom date as a senior, and as he left he said, `I love you Mamaw and Papaw.'

"Even to this day, in front of his football buddies, he says it."

When Tank was about 15, his aunt Missy witnessed a scene that she's sure would embarrass him now. Madison was junior-high age and was in the yard practicing baton twirling.

She was getting frustrated, when Tank walked up and said, "Here, give me the baton."

Says Missy, "He tossed it up, turned around and did a spin, and then caught it like it was nothing – like he'd been taking baton lessons."

At the risk of overanalyzing, that moment might sum up a lot of what Tank Whaley is about:

First, there is the showman and the lack of "macho" inhibitions that might keep other teen boys from grabbing a baton.

But there's also that hand-eye coordination, the natural athleticism, and the competitive streak that certainly spoke to him as he watched Madison struggle: I can do that, let me try.

Of all the traits Tank developed as a child, though, Rich astutely picks out one that is rare and more subtle.

It was on those occasions when he didn't succeed, or when he wasn't given a chance to do what he wanted to do, that his father marveled the most.

"The thing that impresses me the most is how he's able to deal with the disappointments and the downers in sports and life," Rich says. "Somehow, he is able to let it go, not dwell on it, and focus on what he has to do for his team, family and friends."

That would serve him well. At this point in our story, he was heading into high school, which would prove to be another mostly positive experience.

So it's still a few years down the road yet, but eventually Tank would get plenty of opportunities to handle disappointment.

CHAPTER 4:
Tiger Pride

If there were a Mount Rushmore for old-school football coaches, the featured faces might be Woody Hayes, Bear Bryant, Vince Lombardi and Bob Lutz.

Lutz has been the Ironton High mentor for 35 years, and it's probably not too much of a stretch to suggest that every forward pass he's called, he's done so reluctantly. A change-up, you might say.

"We still line up in a T (formation) to start with," Lutz said. "Continuity has always been our biggest thing – continuity and execution. We try to control the line of scrimmage and move the ball inside."

Ironton averages about eight or 10 throws a game.

Lutz is famous for his preseason conditioning sessions – known simply as Physical Fitness.

Ironton Tribune sports editor Jim Walker remembers a former Tigers player coming back to town after going through Marine Corps basic training.

How was it, asked Walker.

It wasn't too bad, the kid replied. Physical Fitness was harder.

Given that throwback style, it seems altogether appropriate that the Tigers play in 82-year-old Tanks Memorial Stadium, under that distinctive canopy roof and amongst the black-and-white ghosts of the old Tankmen. Lutz and Ironton High are honoring their football heritage properly, except that the Tanks of the 1920s ran a more wide-open offense.

Enough of the jokes, though, because however Lutz chooses to do it, it has worked. From their inception in 1902 through the 1960s, the Tigers had a decent if unspectacular program, with a .531 win percentage.

They had some memorable players. George "Lefty" McAfee was All-Ohio in 1935, then All-American at Duke and eventually All-NFL with the Chicago Bears. He was inducted into the Pro Football Hall of Fame in 1966.

Coy Bacon played for Ironton in 1960, then enjoyed a standout NFL career.

But the program was middling, for the most part, until Lutz took over in 1972. In his first 12 seasons, Ironton was never worse than 8-2. One of his best players in those early years was lineman Ken Fritz, who would go on to an All-American career at Ohio State.

But because of an infamous incident in the Gator Bowl in 1978, Fritz still gets referred to as "the guy who held back Woody Hayes after he punched that Clemson player."

Anyway, the program took off. In the 1980s, the Tigers were 103-12-2. Lutz has taken the team to 25 playoff appearances and eight state finals, winning two titles. In his 35 seasons, Ironton has lost 70 games.

The point is, he is a coaching legend. So even if his playbook seems scratched into stone tablets, nobody is going to question him.

And therefore, his rule that no freshmen play is a hard and fast one. He bent it once, in 1996, when he had a weak group of juniors and seniors. The Tigers went 3-7 anyway, Lutz's only losing season.

He swore off playing freshmen ever again, even if in the fall of 1999, one particular freshman certainly appeared able to contribute.

Tank Whaley was in junior high when his grandfather, Tommy Tipton, who served as his de facto sports advisor, realized the stocky kid could really benefit from some proper weight training.

It just so happened that a former record-holding powerlifter lived three doors down from Tank's house on Woodland Drive. Now retired from competition, Larry Browning was training his grandson, Jasun Walker, and a small group of other kids.

"I remember (Tommy) saying, 'If you want to be the best at football, you've got to start lifting, you can't just be lazy, it's not just going to come to you,'" Tank says.

The kid said sure, whereupon Tommy said, "You're going to call him and ask."

Tank wondered why Tommy couldn't call him, but his grandfather insisted that Tank initiate the contact.

"I think he was trying to start that manly 'You need to be a man,' type thing," Whaley recalls. "Take responsibility."

So he did, and Browning readily agreed to help him. For the next few years, Browning would pick Tank up in the evenings, three days a week, and take him across the river to Kentucky to a gym.

Browning taught Tank the proper lifting techniques, but he also tried to work on the kids' mindsets, as well. He stressed positive attitudes, but he found he didn't have to teach Tank a whole lot of that – he already had it.

"He was a coachable kid," Browning says. "He'd do anything I'd tell him to do, and he'd do his very best and do it right. He had good work habits. I really enjoyed being with him, he's a fine young man."

It's like his stepfather, Dave, said: As a kid, Tank always tried to please. Whaley's aunt, Missy Leonard, stresses that character trait, as well.

"He worries about everything, he worries what you think," Missy says. "He just wants to make a good impression. He'll ask you, 'How do you think that went?'"

After a year or two with Browning, Whaley was heading into high school and benching more than 300 pounds.

At Ironton High School, as with many football programs, special recognition is awarded to those who reach certain lifting goals. Ironton's coaches give out "Iron Man" T-shirts to those who can bench 300 pounds or squat 400.

Lutz was teaching physical education to a class of freshman one day, and the class was working on the incline bench press.

Lutz said to Tank, "Why don't you put 135 on there, can you do that?"

Um, yeah, he could do that. He went ahead and benched 300 that day.

"I think (Lutz) liked it," Whaley says. "He was kind of like, 'Whoa, who is this guy?'"

Terry Parker, who coached Tank on his freshman football team that fall, saw the feat. After class, he gave Tank his Iron Man T-shirt – but he still only played freshman ball.

That fall, the varsity Tigers went 7-3 in the regular season, but then steamed through playoff wins over Cincinnati Wyoming,

49

Cincinnati Indian Hill and Youngstown Cardinal Mooney to reach their eighth state title game. They had won championships in 1979 and 1989, so historical symmetry suggested another was on the way in 1999.

They led Sandusky Perkins, 14-10, with 41 seconds left. But on the fourth-and-1 from his own 29-yard line, Lutz elected to go for it. The back was stuffed, and Perkins scored to snatch a 16-14 win.

"My kids didn't lose the game," Lutz told *The Associated Press*. "It was the dumb coach who lost the game."

Never mind the Tigers had gone 8-for-8 on fourth-down tries the week before. It was galling to Lutz because he had lost heart-breakers in the state finals before. One of the most notable was in 1993, when Wauseon tried and missed a last-second game-win-ning field goal attempt, only to see Ironton whistled for roughing the kicker. The kid made his second try.

Tank's freshman team went undefeated that fall, so it's fair to suggest that a few of them might have made a difference on the varsity club. But rules are rules, so Whaley and his teammates would have to wait until 2000 to take their shot at bringing glory to the community.

By 2000, Ironton – and for that matter, Lawrence County and the entire Appalachian region – had been struggling for decades. The demise of the iron, steel and coal industries is a familiar storyline by now, but that shouldn't trivialize how difficult times have been for those communities built on manufacturing jobs that suddenly disappeared in the latter half of the 20th century.

The population of Lawrence County is both shrinking and ag-ing. Kids graduating from high school no longer can count on finding stable, well-paying jobs nearby. Those who go off to col-lege most often don't come back.

Since 1980, the county has lost about 1 percent of its people. In 2006, the number of residents 18 and under was 22.9 percent, compared to 24.1 statewide. Residents 65 or older numbered 14.5 percent, compared to 13.3 in Ohio.

The poverty level was 18.9 percent in 2000 – well above Ohio's 10.6.

Ironton even lost its hospital, although there are several across the river in Kentucky that employ many Ironton residents.

"The town is getting sucked dry," Tank says.

The Tiptons' store and bakery were not immune. As an independent store owner, Tommy Tipton found fewer and fewer warehouses from which to buy. They were all being gobbled up by the Wal-Marts and Giant Eagles and Krogers of the world.

He also was having a difficult time with staffing.

"The biggest problem was finding people willing to work," Tipton said. "When you've got a community that's losing young people, you don't have new people coming in to train. And it's hard work, working at a scratch bakery. It's six days a week, 12 hours a day, all night long."

His workforce shrank. Those that remained, including Whaley's mother, Tammy Vogelsong, worked that much harder.

Anyone who is familiar with hard-hit blue-collar towns like Ironton knows that many residents transfer their hopes and dreams to the local high school sports teams. Success on the field helps restore their morale and pride.

The people of Ironton look to their Tigers, as Billy Joel sings, "to forget about life for awhile."

"It's kind of a fading town," says Lutz, who graduated from Ironton's St. Joseph High, "and our big thing down through the years was Friday night. People rallied around that. They went to the road games and the playoff games. They always traveled real well and always tailgated."

He recalls one year, after losing in the state semifinals, his brother asked him, "What the heck am I going to do next week?"

Dave Coburn played for Ironton in the early 1990s and now is an assistant coach.

"There's nothing here," he says of the town. "Everything is about football Friday nights. You might have 15 or 20 old people watching practice each day – rain, sleet or snow – and these are not parents, just fans. And that's how it has been for 30-some years."

Boys from Ironton grow up wanting to add their own small brick in the wall of tradition.

"It's THE thing in Ironton: If you're a guy, you play football," says Chad Parker, one of Tank's best friends and a former Tigers teammate. "You're born and bred with it. You always wanted to be on that field in front of the whole town. You wanted to be successful, and everyone around you wanted you to be successful."

The townspeople had always been tough, from the mining and smelting days, through the Depression and the floods. Economic struggle was just another tool that served to fine-tune a hard-nosed community personality that served the football team well.

Mike Burcham, an Ironton assistant coach and former athletic director, describes a typical Tigers player in this manner:

"Like all river cities, we have tough kids who have been through tough times," he says. "They don't have a whole lot given to them. Some of their parents have a little bit, and a lot don't. They grow up and have to fend for themselves, and they're tough and strong."

Tammy does a great job describing the Ironton football player's mentality:

"'You can cleat me all the way up my back,'" she says. "'I'll heal, but we've got to get that touchdown.' That's the way it is down here."

The Tigers never made it back to the state finals in Tank's three years on varsity, but they qualified for the playoffs every year and compiled a 29-6 record (25-3 in the regular season).

Now a muscular 5-foot-11, 270 pounds, Tank quickly established himself as a dominant offensive and defensive tackle.

He scrapped every moment of every play as if his life depended on it.

"Very strong and quick," Lutz says. "He always played hard. He'd come off the ball and stick his face right in your numbers. Whatever you asked him to do, he'd do it."

Opponents learned to game plan for the undersized, tenacious kid.

"All the teams scouted us, so 99 percent of the time he was matched up against the other team's best kid – monsters, 300-plus pounders," Tommy Tipton says, "and Tyler always did the job."

Well, almost always. Lutz tells an endearing story of a game against Belfry, Kentucky, in which Tank was struggling against a 340-pound offensive tackle. While on the sideline for a breather, Lutz asked his standout lineman how he was doing.

"He said, 'Coach, I can't move him, he's too big,'" Lutz recalls. "He would tell you honestly."

In his sophomore year of 2000, Ironton went 9-1, won its playoff opener and then lost to Licking Valley in the second round.

The next season would be better. The Tigers featured a powerful offensive and defensive line that included Whaley, his buddy Chad Parker and Roman Fry, who currently is a standout at Clemson.

"We all benched 350, squatted 400," Whaley says.

They were 9-0 and ranked No. 2 in *The Associated Press* Division IV poll when they traveled to Columbus to take on DeSales, a perennial power in Division III, one classification bigger than Ironton.

The teams meet often, and even though the Tigers rarely beat the Stallions, the series has accomplished what Lutz wanted: His team does not ring up many cheap victories against inferior opposition. You only get better by playing better teams.

Ironton had beaten DeSales in 2000, and in 2001, DeSales again had its hands full with the Tigers. At 5-4, the belief was the Stallions had to beat Ironton to make the playoffs.

Whaley and Parker, close friends who played next to each other on offense – tackle and guard – have fond memories of what happened on that frigid November day.

"They were stacked, loaded," Parker recalls. "Tank and I had this pretty good athlete across from us, and we just doubled down on him. One of us would cut him and the other would take him high, and we switched up the whole game.

"We wore him out, and after the game he came up and congratulated us. That's one of those moments we still talk about when we get together."

Whaley said the Tigers had drives of 89 and 91 yards en route to the 20-10 victory.

DeSales squeaked into the playoffs, anyway, and ended up nearly winning a championship. The Stallions lost in overtime to Mentor Lake Catholic to finish 9-6.

Ironton won the poll championship, then won its playoff opener. Arch-rival Portsmouth was next. The Tigers had won a regular-season meeting, 16-15.

Rather than have the Ohio high school association choose a neutral site a good distance away, Portsmouth and Ironton officials agreed to have a coin toss, with the winner hosting the game at its own stadium.

Despite winning the flip, Ironton lost the game, 35-27, to finish 11-1.

The 2001 club would be the best of Whaley's three teams. In his senior season, the Tigers were not as loaded. Lutz moved his standout lineman around a lot, based on the opponent. Tank played some defensive end and even a little bit at linebacker.

The Tigers went 8-3, losing again early in the playoffs. Lutz commented that if he could've just cloned Whaley, they might have fared better.

Coburn, who served as the team trainer during Tank's career, said that despite how hard he played, he never suffered a notable injury.

"He had a fractured little toe one time," Coburn says, "but I never saw him have to come out of a game, not one time. And I never heard the kid complain about anything, ever."

Tyler, now called "Tank," played offensive and defensive line in high school. Here he celebrates a sack of Covington (Kentucky) Holmes quarterback Brandent Englemon. (Family photo)

Tank's senior season included one moment that's worth remembering. Ironton was hosting Covington (Kentucky) Holmes, which featured a standout quarterback, Brandent Englemon.

The family has a photo of Tank standing over Englemon after a sack, flexing and hollering in a rare moment of exultation.

Five years later, the two players would meet again.

All through high school, baseball still had a powerful grip on Tank's heart. No doubt, it was his favorite sport.

The prowess he showed as a kid – the mythical bat-splittings, the pool-earning taters – continued through his Ironton High career. Whaley was a slick-fielding first baseman who could hit for average and power.

Once again, his grandfather Tommy Tipton tells the best stories.

Like the time Tank hit a shot into the outfield gap and made it clear that he was going to try for an inside-the-park home run. This is a 270-pounder, keep in mind, who hit people for a living on the football field.

"For a big boy, he could run," Tipton says, "and coming around third, he sounded like a freight train. The ground was shaking. That catcher wanted no part of (Tank), because if he was coming at you, he was going to kill you. So nobody caught the throw."

Or the time on a spring-break trip when the opposing team, wise to Whaley's power and figuring he would struggle with breaking stuff, brought in a curveball specialist just to pitch to him.

"He parked one past the tennis courts," Tipton says. "They didn't throw him a curve again."

Tank was having a ball. He and his good buddy Matthew White batted third and fourth in the Tigers' lineup and fancied themselves as "bash brothers" in the mold of Mark McGwire and Jose Canseco of the late-1980s Oakland A's.

"There were numerous times we hit back-to-back home runs," Whaley says. "Up through high school, I probably had better memories in baseball than in football."

His mother remembers a moment during a game in Portsmouth that once again demonstrated her son's competitive streak.

"He was playing first base and a ball was hit foul, way over there," she says. "He was determined to get it and end that inning, so he leaned over the fence – took out the fence, cracked the fence in half – but he came up with it."

Tammy says she was back at that field two years later, and the fence was still cracked.

In his senior season, Tank batted .424 with eight home runs and 31 RBI. For his career, he swatted 17 homers, which puts him tied for second on Ironton's all-time list, behind Bill Klaiber's 19.

He also hit over .400 all three seasons on varsity.

Meanwhile – and we're not making this up – the kid was earning a 3.958 grade-point average. He got exactly one B in high school, either in Spanish or calculus, he can't recall.

Amazingly, though, that GPA ranked him 11th in a class of about 100. Oh, and he was his class president...all four years.

As Tank Whaley was putting the finishing touches on his senior baseball season, the logical question became where was he going to college, and would he play sports there?

Clearly he would have loved to play college baseball. But Ironton is a funny sports town. It has that reputation for producing hard-nosed football players, but the baseball program doesn't attract much attention. The coaches don't seem to go out of their way to invite scouts or college recruiters, either.

It's as if the town's love affair with football can't handle competition.

So despite his prodigious power, it became clear to Whaley that football was his future. Now the issue was where he would play.

Tank had a thought bouncing around in his head. For awhile, he kept it to himself, because it was kind of crazy.

But looking back now, his buddy Chad Parker realizes that once that thought occurred to Whaley, it was as good as done.

"Once he sets his mind on something, he does not veer off that path," Parker says. "He will get the job done and achieve his goals, and that's it."

What Tank Whaley had decided was that he was going to play football for Ohio State. As Parker said, it was a done deal, even if Ohio State didn't know it yet.

CHAPTER 5:
"If You Had a Neck"

Tommy Tipton says his grandson needed an agent in high school. With all due respect, a witch doctor might have served Tank Whaley better.

Never mind the eligibility issues, the best agent in the universe would have had trouble convincing a major college coach to take an offensive lineman who was a shade under 6 feet tall.

Like many others who knew of Whaley's strength, heart and determination, this frustrated Tipton.

"There are things you are born with other than height," he says. "But he didn't have that, so he wasn't going to get looked at no matter how talented he was."

He's right, and that's where the witch doctor would come in handy – someone who could break the powerful spell that height, weight, 40-yard dashes and other "measurables" have on coaches, scouts and recruitniks.

Whenever people discuss the business of predicting which high-school players will be collegiate stars, or which college players will make it in the pros, they always refer to the process as an "inexact science."

That's an oxymoron. Science by definition deals with provable facts. There's nothing inexact about it.

In reality, evaluating talent is something far less than inexact. It's an educated guess. You can base it on size, weight, speed and strength. But equally important are some of those traits that Tipton mentioned, things such as inner drive, intelligence and character.

Nowadays, coaches try to dig into those topics. They talk to teachers, professors and strength coaches. They do background checks and Wonderlic tests.

And still, they get it wrong. A lot.

I spent five years covering the NFL, and I was always amazed at how often teams screwed up their top draft choices.

Here you had dozens of scouts and coaches spending months upon months scouring film, touring college campuses, timing and interviewing. Owners of franchises that are worth nearly a billion dollars pay this small army of people healthy salaries to make good draft decisions. And still, it was little better than a 50-50 proposition in the end.

So why should we expect anything more from college coaches, who have a harder job trying to judge younger players, some of whom play against inferior competition?

A big-time program such as Ohio State doesn't need to adjust its ideal size-speed template. Maybe a little. If the coaches feel a kid has some good "intangibles," maybe they would take a 6-foot quarterback, or a 6-2 lineman.

But there's no reason for the Buckeyes or Gators or Longhorns to stretch those boundaries too far, to take a 5-10 quarterback or a 6-foot lineman. Too big of a gamble can cost a coach his job.

So it's no one's fault, really, that Tank Whaley was not offered a scholarship. And the fact that Whaley ended up succeeding at Ohio State hasn't turned the recruiting industry on its ear. Good for him, coaches say. He's an exception to the rule.

There is a Division I box, and guys like Whaley will never fit into it.

He got that point pretty clearly by the end of 2002, his senior football season at Ironton High. He had no scholarship offers.

Rich Whaley, Tank's father, figured that would be the case ever since he had accompanied Tammy, Dave and Tank to several college camps the previous summer. At West Virginia and even at Miami (Ohio), a mid-major program, Rich looked around at the number of 6-7, 340-pound linemen and thought to himself, "There's no way he will be a Division I lineman."

He thought maybe Tank's only shot at the big time would be by playing fullback, or maybe he could play on the line at a Division II or III school.

Rich didn't tell his son that, but others weren't as tactful. Clemson coach Tommy Bowden came to Ironton while he was recruiting Roman Fry, Tank's fellow lineman. The Ironton coaches recommended that Bowden check out Whaley while he was there.

Bowden took one look at Tank and told him, "If you had a neck, you'd be tall enough, but you don't have a neck."

Next on the list of options was heading to a Division III school, all of which would welcome a First Team All-Ohioan no matter what size he was.

Whaley could have his pick of those colleges, and he decided to visit Wittenberg University in Springfield, Ohio. The Tigers have a proud tradition – more wins than any other Division III program in the nation (671), including five national titles.

He visited the campus and liked what he saw. Then he and a Wittenberg offensive lineman who was acting as host sat down and watched some Tigers highlight tapes.

Whaley asked the guy how many people came to watch their games.

Probably three or four hundred, came the answer.

"I was like, `Parents? And then you have fans?'" Tank recalls. "And he said, `No, that's everybody.'"

At Ironton, the average home crowd was probably 5,000. For a big rival like Portsmouth or Wheelersburg, it might swell closer to 10,000.

Playing in front of a few hundred, by comparison, "would be a letdown, I think," Whaley says. "That would be opposite of the direction I wanted to go."

Before dismissing the Tigers out of hand, though, he talked to Drew Mains, who had been a year ahead of him at Ironton High and had just finished his freshman year at Wittenberg.

"I said, 'How is it up there?' and he said, 'Tank, I'll tell you one thing: You've got to buy your own cleats,'" Whaley said.

After being cheered by adoring throngs in Ironton, the small-college level clearly would be a culture shock to him. So much for Division III.

That left one other path – walking on to a big school without a scholarship. Dave and Tammy assured Tank they could afford to pay for it. It wouldn't be easy, but they could do it.

Whaley's high school coach, Bob Lutz, was a Marshall University graduate, so he arranged a visit for Tank and his teammate and neighbor, Matthew White. The visit went well enough and both players were assured they could walk on.

But by this point, in March, Tank was thinking that if he had to walk on somewhere, why not aim high? Why not follow the dream of being an Ohio State Buckeye?

About this time, Lutz was in the Tipton family store one day and ran into Tammy. He asked how Tank had liked his visit to Marshall.

Tammy assured him Tank liked it fine.

When Lutz asked Tammy what Tank planned to d o, she replid that since he's always like Ohio State, he decided to apply there for school.

Rather than be taken aback or scoff, what Lutz did next is a measure of how much he believed in his hard-nosed two-way lineman.

"He pulled out his cell phone and called (Ohio State) on the spot, right in front of Mom," Whaley says. "And that's how this whole process started."

The man on the receiving end of Lutz's call that day was one of his former players who had left Ironton and made quite a name for himself.

Mark Snyder played for the Tigers in the early 1980s and ended up as a standout safety at nearby Marshall University. In 1987, Snyder intercepted 10 passes, a Thundering Herd record stll to-day.

He then embarked on a coaching career that wound through Central Florida, Youngstown State (under Jim Tressel) and Minnesota. When Tressel was hired at Ohio State in 2001, he brought Snyder in as a defensive backs coach.

Snyder and the Buckeyes were just coming off their 2002 national championship, which further cemented his status as an Ironton favorite son. His wife, the former Beth Molter, is a native as well.

So he understands and respects Lutz and Tiger football. When Lutz talked to him about Tank Whaley, Snyder agreed to see what he could do.

Not long after, Snyder was in Ironton, where he was being honored during a basketball game. Whaley introduced himself. Snyder gave him his card and told him to call the staffer who handles the process and paperwork that comes with being a walk-on.

Tank was invited to come up to Columbus during OSU's spring practice. Snyder would introduce him to the coaches and show him around. He already had mentioned Whaley to Jim Bollman, the Buckeyes' offensive line coach.

Bollman was willing to take a look. His experience with walk-ons generally had been positive – at the time of Whaley's recruitment, walk-on guard Mike Kne was about to be awarded a scholarship and would end up starting in 2004. John Conroy later earned a scholarship and playing time for Bollman, as well.

No doubt, Snyder had told Bollman that Whaley was undersized, but apparently Bollman wasn't prepared for just howundersized.

"He showed up, and Bollman thought he was a little short," Snyder recalls.

Bollman is not a man prone to flowery speech. Of that first impression, he says, "Naturally I was a little concerned about his height, you know?"

At this point, as Whaley's sponsor, so to speak, Snyder was in a position in which he had to decide how far to go to bat for Whaley.

Division I college football teams are allowed to bring 105 players to camp, of which only 85 can be on scholarship. So there are 20 spots for walk-ons. Once the games begin, teams are gradually allowed to add another 15 walk-ons.

Even with 120 spots, though, walk-ons are not accepted willy-nilly. Those players fill valuable roles, particularly on special teams. Generally one of them will end up as the starting long snapper, another as the holder for place kicks or the backup punter.

If nothing else, walk-ons must be able to perform well on scout teams, to effectively prepare the starters for each opponent.

So to make the 105-man camp roster, a walk-on player must be invited.

Snyder was at the fulcrum of this debate. On the one hand, he faced Bollman's skepticism. On the other hand, he was hearing it from his wife and her mother, Margaret Molter.

Tank's mother, Tammy, was a friend of theirs and had made cakes for the Molter family. They were in Snyder's ear about the Whaley boy.

"They pounded on me," Snyder says. "I said, 'You guys want me to bring (Whaley) up to the staff (for consideration)? He's a 5-11 center.' But they kept saying, 'He's a great kid, he has a huge heart, all those things.'"

Meanwhile, a Wittenberg assistant coach had been calling Whaley persistently. Tank tried to be as polite as possible, but he knew at this point he wasn't going there.

The coach finally asked him what he wanted to do.

"I said I thought I was going to walk on either at Marshall or Ohio State," Whaley recalls. "He said, 'Do you know what you'll have to go through walking on at Marshall or Ohio U?'"

Now, Tank is naturally polite and laid-back. But the coach's inadvertent slip prompted Whaley to gently but firmly interrupt the guy.

"I was like, 'No, I'm pretty sure I said Ohio State.'"

That didn't stop the coach.

"He couldn't comprehend that I said Ohio State," Tank says. "He was like, 'There's no way.' He kept saying I could come (to Wittenberg) and play right away, that I would probably be an All-American as a true freshman... blah, blah, blah."

Having grown up a Buckeyes fan and being surrounded by a family full of them, Whaley now had his heart set on OSU. All that was left to learn was whether Ohio State would return the love.

As spring dragged toward summer, roster decisions had to be made. Caught between the women in his family and Bollman's reluctance, Snyder finally called Mike Burcham, a longtime Ironton coach and athletic director.

Like Lutz, Burcham is old-school and no-nonsense. He could be counted on to cut to the chase about Tank Whaley.

Coach Burcham assured Snyder that Tank could play for OSU. When Snyder reminded Burcham that Tank would have to face (OSU defensive linemen) Tim Anderson, Will Smith and Darrion Scott on the scout team., Burcham responded that Tank would not disappoint him.

That was enough for Snyder. He went to bat for Whaley, and Tressel agreed to let him walk on.

The call came to the house while Tank was at baseball practice, sometime in May 2003. Tammy answered. When Tank came home, Tammy was beaming.

"You made it, honey," she said.

"What are you talking about, Mom?"

"You're an Ohio State Buckeye. Coach Snyder just called and said you had a spot."

They hugged and hollered together. As it turns out, Snyder had forged a compromise. Whaley had a spot, but not on the 105 that could come to fall camp. He would join the team after the first game, with the next wave of walk-ons.

Still, it was a spot. And needless to say, that ended any other thoughts of what Whaley was going to do for college.

"Your family is all Buckeye fans, you're an extreme Buckeye fan, to be from Ohio, a town that's not that big – I mean, what's better?" Tank says. "So as soon as that came out of (Snyder's) mouth, 'You've got a spot,' it was done. I knew what I was doing."

Word travels fast in a small town. The very next day, on his way to baseball practice, Whaley drove by Linn's Sporting Goods downtown. He did a double-take. On the marquee, it read, "Congratulations Tank Whaley, the newest Buckeye."

The reaction around Ironton was interesting. Folks were excited that one of their own was heading to Ohio State, of course. But many had their doubts that Tank would ever see the light of day. Nothing personal, of course, just a recognition of the cold reality of what often happens when dreamers hit the big city.

"Most of us thought he would go someplace small and play," said Jim Walker, *Ironton Tribune* sports editor. "But if (OSU) is what he wanted to try, well, good for him. Everybody was like, 'Well, good for him, good luck, we'll cheer you all the way.'

"It wasn't anything negative, but I don't think anybody expected great things. We all knew he wasn't six feet tall. But then again, we knew what type of kid he was, and what a hard worker he was."

His buddy Chad Parker says, "I was behind him 100 percent. I knew he'd make the team – there wasn't a doubt in my mind, with his strength and determination."

Like Whaley's father, though, Parker thought maybe Tank should try to play fullback rather than the line.

"He had good footwork and size for that position," Parker says. "I told him he should mention something to one of the coaches and see what they say."

Even some of his family members wondered what he was getting into.

Tank's uncle Andy Whaley remembered his neighbor asking him, "Do you think Tyler will ever play?"

Andy said he didn't think so.

"I could see him running onto the field and dressing for the games," he said. "But I figured that would be the highlight. Whatever else he got would be gravy."

Tommy Tipton was concerned about Whaley getting buried by the politics of being a walk-on. He worried that even if Tank outplayed a scholarship player, "would there be that recognition of what he could do? Would anybody see that?"

It's an understandable concern but actually, the college game provides more opportunity for unheralded players to rise.

In the NFL, no matter how often coaches trot out that tired, "the-best-players-will-play" line, everyone knows the high draft pick is going to get first crack at the job over the undrafted free agent.

Much of that has to do with economic factors. That top pick is virtually bulletproof for a few years, simply because cutting him and his big contract means taking a bath on the salary cap.

In college, there is not that complicating issue. If a stud recruit doesn't pan out, sure, the coach might take some heat for not developing him, or even for recruiting him in the first place. But there's no real reason not to elevate a deserving walk-on to a starting spot.

Like everyone else, Rich Whaley figured his son's determination would allow him to stick on the roster.

"What I wasn't sure about was how he would handle getting kicked around sitting in the background," he said.

He'd find out soon enough.

Tank was fully aware of what he was getting himself into. He recognized he would have to work harder than he ever had to compete with bigger and faster athletes – and that would be just in practice.

At that point, he hooked up with Dave Coburn, the Ironton trainer, who also worked as a personal trainer. The two would spend the summer trying to whip him into better shape.

Coburn said that at the time, Whaley had 25 percent body fat, hardly ideal. He estimates Whaley could run no better than a 5.3- or 5.4-second 40-yard dash. Division I linemen probably should be closer to 5.1.

As the two worked out a program for the summer, Coburn sensed that getting into better physical condition might also help Whaley mentally.

"I think he needed a little confidence," Coburn says. "There was a little doubt in his mind, as well as in others' minds, that he could do this."

The first thing Coburn and Whaley tackled was that body fat. Tank sweated through interval training on a treadmill, simulating the fast-slow-fast bursts of a series of football plays. As he lost fat, he would gain muscle mass and his speed would improve.

To further work on speed, Coburn strapped ropes and a parachute around him, as well as a weight vest, and had Whaley run. Cone drills were included to work on his cutting and agility.

At the same time, Tank worked hard on long snapping. Snyder had mentioned that role as an opportunity for playing time. Whaley had never done it in a game, but after hours and hours of practice, he felt good about his ability.

By the end of the summer of 2003, Coburn and Whaley both felt their work had paid off. Coburn would not check Whaley's body fat again until 2004, when he had been in the Ohio State weight and conditioning program for a year, but when they did, it was 19 percent.

As the day for reporting to Ohio State neared, Tank said he started to feel a sense of responsibility. The people of Ironton, struggling with a sense that their town's best days were behind them, looked to their former Tigers players with pride and hope. They wanted someone to point to on their television screens and say, "He's from Arnt-n, you know."

Adding to the burden was that others had failed before him. Jermon Jackson was a candidate for Ohio's Mr. Football award as an Ironton running back in the early 1990s. He headed to Ohio State apparently destined to be the next Eddie George. He didn't make it through four years.

Redgie Arden had earned a Buckeyes scholarship in 2001, but by 2003, his record already was checkered with injuries and off-field problems. He wouldn't last in Columbus much longer, either.

"The town's image was messed up, and to the outside world, it didn't have a good reputation," Whaley said. "That gave me the motivation to keep things under control and get the town's image back."

Larry Browning, his old weight-lifting coach, came by the Whaley house to give Tank a pep talk.

"I said, 'You're going to have to fight the wars, you're not going to be given anything, and you're going to have to earn everything you get,'" Browning recalls. "But I also told him he had a great opportunity to show what you can do."

As always, though, the counsel he kept closest to his heart belonged to his mother. The two always had a warm and special bond, more like brother-sister at times than mother-son.

When he confided his doubts to Tammy – Am I getting in over my head, Ma? – they talked until both were comfortable with the bottom line.

"I'm going to Ohio State, and I'm going to play football, and if football doesn't work out, at least I tried it," Whaley says, describing his mindset. "If it doesn't work out, I'm still here for school, and I'll graduate and get my degree.

"And that's all Mom ever told me: 'Just go try it. If they don't want you or you can't do it, so be it, but don't give up.'"

CHAPTER 6:
Out of the Picture

According to the 2003 Ohio State football media guide, Tank Whaley was not a Buckeye.

Oh, he spent the season with them, all right, redshirting and working on the scout team. But there is no mention of him in the media guide – not a photo, not a bio, he's not even on the roster.

That's called starting at the bottom, or as a former high-school teacher of mine liked to say, "Lower than the sweat on a snake's belly in a wagon rut."

The depths from which he had to climb hit Whaley hard that August.

Remember, he was not on the 105-man roster that was allowed to participate in preseason camp. Rather, he would join the team the week after their first game, which was August 30 against Washington.

Like all incoming freshmen, Whaley had to attend orientation. It was the first week of August, and Tank and his mother came to Columbus. They were wandering around campus and decided to swing by Ohio Stadium.

It just happened to be Photo Day, an annual event in which the team gets its group and individual photos taken. It draws a big crowd of family and friends, as well as reporters, who are allowed a rare opportunity to interview any player they want.

Tank and Tammy sat up in the stands, watching the photographer gather the players in the bleachers for the picture.

It was a jarring moment.

"I'm not even in the team picture, here I am up in the stands just watching," Whaley said. "My mom, of course, didn't like it. She wasn't crying, but she was emotional."

They got up and walked out.

"I just wanted to leave," he said. "That was really gut-wrenching."

The next few weeks didn't help. As the Buckeyes continued to practice, Tank followed their progress through news reports – the position battles, the scrimmages, the excitement building for a veteran-laden OSU team looking to defend its national title.

Whatever sense of euphoria and accomplishment he had felt back in the spring had vanished. He had been assured that he had a spot. Logically, nothing had changed, but emotionally, he was a mess.

"Here's this team I'm going to be on, and I have no part in it right now," he said. "For the first time, I've gone from being a real good athlete to now I'm starting to question my abilities, like, `Can I even play at this level? I'm not even on the team yet, am I going to be able to do this?'"

The doubts grew as he looked back with an objective eye at how he had landed the roster spot in the first place: In reality, it was a favor, from OSU assistant coach Mark Snyder to his former high school coach, Bob Lutz.

Snyder was taking an undersized kid on Lutz's word.

"So I get accepted, kind of, as a preferred walk-on through some ties," Whaley thought to himself. "They don't really want me here, but somehow I'm here, so. . . ."

So, at that low point, Whaley came up with a coping mechanism that would greatly comfort him over the new few years.

He set a goal – a small goal and only one, not a whole series. If he accomplished the first, he would set another.

His first goal?

"Prove to myself I belonged here."

Meanwhile, there was turmoil back on the home front in Ironton, as well.

After years of struggle, Tommy Tipton was faced with the reality that he would have to close his store and bakery. He was down to one warehouse to buy from, and his workforce was shrinking, with no young people around to take over.

He had been sinking his own money into the place for a few years. Six employees now were doing the work once handled by 13. It wasn't fair.

Tommy knew his business was an Ironton institution, founded in 1935 by his father and uncles. It was beloved as a scratch bakery and an independent grocer, one of those increasingly rare places that had an on-site butcher, among other amenities.

Generations of folks had grown up with Tipton's fresh-baked specialties. Since Tammy started decorating cakes in the early 1980s, hundreds of families would go nowhere else for their birth-day and wedding-cake needs.

"I took it as far as I could take it," Tommy says, still speaking a bit defensively, even nearly five years later. "I probably held on four years longer than I should have."

His wife Dotty says, "He felt dedicated to his employees, that was the hard part. He had several longtime employees."

Still, a good businessman like Tommy knew it was time to go. Tipton's closed for good in 2003 after 68 years of feeding and serv-ing the people of Ironton, through depressions and wars, booms and busts.

The impact is hard to fathom for those who didn't grow up with Tipton's.

Says Tommy, "I don't like to talk about it, even now."

Townspeople actually grieved, like a beloved family member had died. They came to Tammy and Dave's house, sat at the din-ing-room table and cried with Tammy.

And really, they still aren't over it.

Virginia Bryant, a town historian, speaks longingly of Tipton's hamburger buns. Folks would eat them plain, like dinner rolls. Others talk about the crème horns, sort of like a homemade Twinkie, only better. Everyone has his or her favorite.

Few people, though, were affected by the closing as much as Tammy. She had worked there for 20 years, pouring her consid-erable heart into producing beautiful cakes for her customers.

"I was panicked, depressed," she says. "I was like, 'What do I do?' I was 40 years old and I didn't know anything else."

Adding to her misery was that this happened right around the time Tank was heading off to college. Her husband Dave had a steady job, but the loss of income could not have come at a worse time.

The solution came from the townsfolk, who simply would not accept going anywhere else for their cakes.

"(Tammy) was in such demand, people were going crazy," says her mother, Dotty Tipton. "They were like, 'What are we going to do?'"

They called Tammy at home, begging her to do this cake or that cake for them.

Finally she and Dave came up with the idea to keep her part of the business alive. They knocked down a deck and built an extra room on the house. They purchased a commercial-grade oven and got the proper permits to operate a bakery out of their home.

Later in 2003, Tipton's Traditions Inc. was open for business and soon was going strong.

"Customers just kept calling," Tammy says. "They dug me out of (her depression). They really saved the day."

The second-ranked Buckeyes handled Washington in their opener, 28-9. The next day, Whaley and a small group of fellow walk-ons were finally allowed to join the team.

That day was more awkward than triumphant, though. The team already was a tight one, as they returned 20 starters from 2002.

And as usual, they had been sequestered in their hotel through camp, bonding through two-a-days, meals and video games in the evenings.

In walked Tank Whaley, Daniel Dye, D'Angelo Haslem, Dimitrios Makridis and Ryan Franzinger. They might as well have been wearing jerseys that said "No Name Scrub."

"It's one of the loneliest feelings in the world to not know any-body," Tank said. "You've got your walk-on buddies, but for the rest of the team, you're just kind of tagging along. They had no clue who I was."

Although he had been billed as a center and possibly long snap-per coming in, the coaches put him at guard. Center is an impor-tant spot, even on the scout team. The staff didn't want to waste time with a guy they didn't know snapping the ball, possibly fum-bling, not knowing what he's doing.

Whaley was given No. 79. Sitting in the locker room for the first time, he was next to No. 78, fifth-year senior guard Bryce Bishop, who was 6-3, 312 pounds. On the other side was No. 80, third-year sophomore tight end Ryan Hamby, 6-5, 240 pounds.

Bishop and Hamby could have carried on a conversation eye-to-eye, looking right over top of the 5-11 walk-on sitting in be-tween.

Just like that, Tank had gone from being a fan of the Buckeyes to one being of them – sort of.

The new arrivals passed their physicals and were cleared for practice. Since it was a game week, though, and the rest of the team was going full speed, Whaley and the other walk-ons would be eased in for a few days.

So on Tank's first day, he jogged onto the practice field behind the Woody Hayes Athletic Center wearing what they call "shells" – helmet, shoulder pads and shorts.

He stood there watching for a few plays, wondering what to do. Someone, he doesn't remember who, suddenly hollered over to him, "Hey, give me a breather, come on!"

He ran onto the field.

"Everybody else has full pads on, and I have no pants and I don't know what's going on," Whaley says. "First day, I'm nervous."

Mark Dantonio, the defensive coordinator, blew his whistle and started hollering.

"What is he doing, he doesn't even have pants on, for crying out loud!" Dantonio yelled.

Turning to Whaley, he commanded, "Get out."

He wasn't mad at Whaley, really, just upset somebody let the kid play in half a uniform, but it was an inauspicious start.

The first time Tammy came to see her son after he joined the team, she noticed he was unusually quiet around the other players.

This wasn't like Tank. He was an outgoing kid who liked to talk and joke and ham it up. She asked him why he was so quiet.

"I didn't want to come on too strong," he said. "I didn't want to be the loud guy everyone got annoyed with."

He also told his mother that for now, in front of the guys, she should call him Tyler, not Tank. It's sort of a presumptuous-sounding nickname, anyway.

"If I came in and said, 'You can call me Tank,' (players) would be like, 'Who is this young goober who wants to call himself Tank?'"

Eventually, though, the name would follow him. When Snyder talked to Whaley's Ironton High coaches back home, they referred to him as Tank. Soon Snyder found himself doing the same, and at some point he was Tank again. But not yet.

The purpose of the scout team is to simulate the opponent's formations and plays in order to better prepare for what the team will see on game day. All coaches really want from scout teams, though, is what they call "giving us a good look."

They don't want to get their starters hurt in practice, so there is no need for scout teamers to go overboard. Basically, for an offensive lineman like Whaley, the coaches just wanted him to get in position to make a block, to go where the opponent's guard would go and simply get in the defender's way.

But that's not what Tank Whaley was ever about. He knew only one way to play – all out. And after that tough first day, he got his groove back.

"I came in gung-ho, I'm like an engine that didn't ever want to stop," he said.

Now, earlier I made the point that Whaley's story was not exactly a Rudy story, that it went way beyond what the latter ever accomplished. But at this point, a moment occurred for Whaley that almost exactly mimics a scene from Rudy.

Defensive end Will Smith – a star who would be first-round NFL draft pick the following spring – was dropping back into coverage on a zone-blitz play. Whaley, pulling from his guard spot, hit him.

And then, like a Lego, he attached himself to Smith and stuck fast, feet churning furiously.

As Tank remembers it, "He kind of shielded me and held me up, and I kept trying to chop my feet, and he's like, 'What are you trying to do, be an All-American? I stopped, why do you keep trying?'"

Why? Because that's how Whaley practiced.

"Everything was like World War III for me," he said. "It was a cut-throat, live-or-die type of thing. That's how I lived, the whole practice."

Much of that was innate, of course, but Whaley also credits Bob Lutz and his old-school Ironton High football heritage, as well as his mother.

"You get after it, man," Tank says. "It's man-on-man, nose-in-the-mud, deliver-a-blow-before-you-even-look-for-the-ball type of football. You develop that mentality.

"Then you grow up with a mom who's got a lot of heart, who shows you what hard work is. You don't even realize you're taking it all in, but you do. Then you come (to Ohio State) and it comes out almost involuntarily."

Like that play against Will Smith, Whaley just kept coming at the bigger, more accomplished players, day after day.

"I was like that little nuisance," he says. "'OK, yeah, you may knock the crap out of me, but I'm going to come back and hit you again.'

"'Yeah, you knocked me on my butt, but it's not going to bother me.' In my mind, I'm just a walk-on, anyway. 'You should be doing that (dominating), so I'm just going to keep on coming after you.'"

Luckily for him, the veterans on the 2003 defensive line didn't mind. They were a hard-nosed sort, as well – guys like Tim Anderson, a former wrestler from the small town of Clyde, Ohio, for example.

Whaley was not the typical scout-teamer, and he was getting their attention.

"He went after Timmy every day, he never backed down," Snyder said. "I recall vividly Tim came up to me one day, 'Where did you get that little punk from?' (Tank) was a strong kid, he never took a play off, he had all those intangibles."

Kirk Barton was another offensive lineman on the scout team. He came in that fall and redshirted, as well.

"He definitely stood out from the pack," Barton says. "For one thing, he's like 5-10. But then he was a tough kid – he fought, and he really earned a lot of respect by how he acted and carried himself."

Still, games came and went, and the new walk-ons were not yet deemed worthy even of dressing for the games.

As walk-ons, Whaley was allotted two tickets instead of four for scholarship players. He used those two for himself and Tammy. The rest of the family was on their own. When his stepfather, siblings or grandparents could find tickets, they often were scattered in ones and twos around the stadium.

For three weeks, Tank sat in the stands and watched his own team play. Finally, as the 3-0 Bucks prepared for Bowling Green on September 20, word came: Walk-ons would dress.

He will never forget walking into the locker room that morning.

"Just seeing that jersey hanging in the locker with 'Whaley' on the back, you just kind of take a deep breath and say, 'Wow,'" he recalls.

Whaley was undersized for a big-time college football offensive lineman. Warming up for a 2003 game, Whaley (79) is dwarfed by fellow linemen Kirk Barton (74) and T.J. Downing (72). (Family photo)

The next moment, of course, he was taking the field with the team for the first time. Even veteran players struggle to describe what it's like to charge out of the tunnel, into the light and air, with the cavernous sides of Ohio Stadium rising high above on either side.

And then, the sound hits – the clear notes and thumping drums of the marching band and the thunderous roar of 100,000 people, most of whom resemble religious pilgrims rather than spectators, such is their passion.

"There's no better feeling," he said.

Whaley's grandmother, Dotty Tipton, was there that day.

"Seeing him run out on the field, tears were dropping off my face," she said. "I knew Tyler was living his dream. I got so excited just seeing him on the sidelines."

That's where he stayed for the rest of the games, of course, as a redshirt.

But with his first goal out of the way – they didn't spit him out and send him back to Ironton – Whaley quickly found something else to shoot for.

For bowl games, just like coming to preseason camp, teams are limited to dressing 105 players.

"I hope I make the travel squad," he said. "I don't want to be sitting up in the stands."

Had Ohio State beaten Michigan in the regular-season finale that season, the bowl would have been the Sugar, for the national championship. But the Buckeyes fell behind their archrivals early, and a late rally fell short.

The 35-21 defeat is coach Jim Tressel's only loss to the Wolverines in seven tries, and the Buckeyes accepted a Fiesta Bowl bid against Kansas State.

By then, Whaley had carved out a niche for himself. He was quickly becoming the leader of the scout team, and his all-out, all-the-time style was endearing him to the coaching staff.

They used him to help prod the starters when they got a bit lazy in practice.

"He was the guy we went to," Snyder said. "Dantonio and me, we went to Tank and would say, 'We've got to get going, these guys are taking a day off.'"

In the end, it paid off. After only a few months of practice, this too-short, too-slow kid they had never heard of was someone the coaches didn't want to be without.

One day that December, Whaley's offensive line coach, Jim Bollman, called him in to give him the news. "You've made the bowl travel squad," he said.

Tank's first act was to call Tammy to tell her he made the 105.

"I was so proud of myself," Whaley says. "She is always the first one I call. She has always done whatever it took to get me where I was, she was on this ride with me."

He was the same old Tank in bowl practice. Once, he got slammed backward by defensive tackle Darrion Scott. The force broke Whaley's chinstrap and his helmet popped him squarely on the nose.

No big deal, he'd gone through that sort of thing all year. He shoved two cotton balls up his nose to absorb the blood, got a new chinstrap, buckled it up and went right back in.

His teammates looked at him.

"You could tell they were like, 'Are you serious?'" Whaley says.

He was. His first two goals had already been accomplished. As 2004 dawned, he didn't dare set his next goal too high, like actually getting into a game.

Instead he was focused on becoming the best scout-teamer Ohio State had ever seen. And in 2004, he would be in the team picture – literally, at least, if nothing more.

CHAPTER 7:

"Is It Worth It?"

ank Whaley had no idea what to expect when he headed to Jim Bollman's office one morning early in 2004. Under head coach Jim Tressel, every Ohio State player has an individual meeting with a coach in the offseason, usually in February. Juniors and seniors meet with the Big Man himself. All others report to their position coaches.

The point is to discuss each player's status: What role the coaches foresee for him, or what they think he must do to improve.

Players also are asked for their input, and they often turn into wide-ranging general discussions.

Whaley obviously had established himself as a valuable scout-teamer, but even with a lot of turnover on the offensive line – OSU was looking to replace three starters – he realized he was not even remotely in the mix for playing time.

The 2004 media guide contained an outlook for the season. Ten offensive linemen were listed as possibilities to see time at the three open spots, and Whaley wasn't one of them.

So as he and Bollman were talking that day, he thought back to what Mark Snyder had mentioned to him a year earlier as a route to possible playing time: long snapping.

It seemed like a good time to bring that up.

"I've been working on long snapping, I think that's something maybe I can pursue," Tank said.

Bollman said, "To be honest with you, I don't want you over there snapping for half an hour during practice. We need you – you can play. That would be a waste for us to have you over there snapping half the practice when you can be practicing offensive line.

"That's something maybe we can venture into (later), but right now, you just stick to playing offensive line."

It was one those "what did you just say?" moments for Whaley.

If he heard Bollman right, he just saw a ray of light. A waste to long snap? We need you – you can play?

Wow.

"That was the first time I felt, 'OK, maybe he DOES think I can do more than what they showed me from the get-go,'" he said.

Looking back now, Bollman says, "You don't have to be around him very long to see he's a pretty good football player. To be honest, it didn't take very long to see that he was a very competitive guy and a very tough guy."

Tank's immediate reaction after leaving that meeting? He called Tammy, of course.

"They think I can do some stuff," he told his mother. "They want me to actually play."

Maybe this Ohio State thing was going to work out after all.

The morale boost was much needed, because he was enduring plenty of other indignities. Constantly he was reminded of what he was – a walk-on scout-teamer.

In the summer of 2004, Whaley came to the practice facility for a workout. He put his clothes in his locker as usual and headed for the weight room.

He came back to find all his gear stuffed in a mesh gym bag and thrown into another, formerly empty locker.

What's the deal, he asked an equipment guy, slightly perturbed.

Oh, sorry, came the answer. A new guy is coming in, and he's getting your jersey number, so we needed to clear out your locker.

The new guy was 6-5, 280-pound freshman tackle Jon Skinner, a well-regarded recruit from western Pennsylvania. He wanted No. 79, and the pecking order demands that scholarship players get what they want.

That's how Whaley found out he was now No. 54. Even with his realistic outlook and low expectations, this one was tough to take.

"I thought, 'Man, this is how you treat me, after I've given you a whole year (of work)?'" Whaley said.

The 2004 media guide was printed before all the changes were made, obviously. Whaley made the roster this year, at least, but he and Skinner were both listed as No. 79.

Even that scene wasn't as depressing as the one that awaited Tank when he went home to Ironton that offseason. He was out with one of his aunts one night when he struck up a conversation with a guy who might have had one too many drinks.

"He says to me, 'I think it's great you're up there (at OSU). What position are you playing?'" Whaley recalls.

"Offensive line," he said.

"That's good, because in my eyes, you were better on the offensive line in high school, anyway. I'll be straight up with you – you sucked on defense."

"Are you serious?" Tank countered. "You're telling me this face to face, and you're the one with the beer belly and you're still in Ironton. Why would you come up and say that to me?"

A year in obscurity had emboldened his detractors, apparently. But it also strengthened his resolve.

"People say you don't know what you've got to fight for until you're at the bottom," he said. "So being at the bottom of the bottom, looking up at everything, you kind of realize what you've got to do. It's kind of a motivation-type thing, to have people saying, 'You can't do this.'"

Tank visits with his father, Rich Whaley. (Family photo)

Even without the extra grief he took, it was hard enough to be a walk-on.

Of course financially, the difference is vast, that much is obvious. But when you're a walk-on, there are a zillion other reminders of your status as a second-class citizen.

Scholarship players don't pay a dime for tuition or books. They also don't have to stand in line at bookstores – the athletic department sends in each player's needs, like a reserve system, and all he does is stop by and pick the books up.

Scholarship players get a monthly stipend for room and board. If several players live together, there can be a significant amount of leftover cash to use for cell phones, televisions or video games.

The two-ticket limit for walk-ons was a hardship, as well, particularly for a player like Whaley with a large supportive family.

Tammy and Dave of course usually took up the two freebies. Tank's grandparents were left to scramble.

"That was hard for them, because they've been to everything my whole life," Whaley says.

His grandmother, Dotty Tipton, said the people of Ironton often stepped up to help by selling or donating theirs to the family. After awhile, a network of three or four people emerged, and the Tiptons missed very few games.

"That's one thing about living in a community like Ironton, it's small and people know everybody and they just try to help," Tank says. "They knew I always had a ton of family that wanted to go, and they'd just call my mom and say, 'Hey, I've got two tickets.'"

Then there's training table. That's basically a fully-stocked, healthful buffet meal. Scholarship players can be provided one meal for every day that the university's cafeterias are open.

That's probably the most jarring difference if you're a walk-on. After practice and showering, most of the team heads to training table. You head home to whatever is in the fridge, or maybe the Taco Bell drive-thru.

That also was what upset Tammy the most. She is the typical mother-hen type.

"He couldn't eat with the team," she says, still indignant years later. "Here he was, killing himself to be part of the team. He didn't even know how to cook yet, and they're not even feeding him?

"I didn't understand that. That's so sad."

She sent her son food, but she's still on the warpath about it.

"That should change," she said. "The athletic department makes enough money, they could feed all of them. That's a stupid rule – give the kid a baloney sandwich, at least."

Tammy found herself commiserating often with other parents of walk-ons. She articulates one point very well – the sense of entitlement some scholarship players feel.

It's understandable. Blue-chip athletes went through the recruiting process in which the nation's top coaches groveled at their feet. Then they come in and have just about all their needs looked after.

At the very least, even well-grounded scholarship players probably don't appreciate what the life of a walk-on is like.

"I don't think anyone grasps what these kids are doing – getting beat up every day and not getting any benefits," Tammy says. "They're paying for their books and their school just because they want to be a Buckeye. I get so mad at these kids who get wined and dined by the university and have to be talked into coming here. What's wrong with them?"

What was wrong with his mother? That was another question Tank started asking when he saw how exhausted Tammy was when she came to Columbus for his games.

Since the previous year, when she and Dave built a commercial kitchen onto their house and she started her own baking and cake-decorating business, Tammy had been in heavy demand. Her decorating skills were legendary, with people calling in orders all over the Kentucky-Ohio-West Virginia area and beyond.

This was great, of course, in one respect. It made it easier to pay for Tank's tuition bills.

But Tammy can't say no to anyone, particularly because just about everyone who calls is a dear friend.

"She does that all the time," says Dotty, her mother. "Somebody will call for a cake at the last minute, and she'll do it. She's got more work than she can handle."

Dotty helps a few days a week, icing the cakes and leaving them for Tammy to decorate. Dave will deliver cakes or pick up supplies on his days off from Dow Chemical.

Still, Tammy's workload is intense.

"I pretty much live on two, maybe four hours of sleep a night," Tammy says. "I do about 100 to 120 cakes a week. I bake all night and decorate all day. Tyler gets panicked, he sees how fast I'm aging. I don't feel good, I don't have the energy I used to have."

Weekends, of course, are when most people want birthday or

wedding cakes, so Tammy has to work around the clock to be able to take a game Saturday off. Dave says it was not unusual for her to arrive in Columbus having not slept since Wednesday.

"Mom will come up, get through the whole game and go out to eat afterward, she'll be laughing and carrying on," Tank says, "but then we'll go back to my apartment, and she sits on the couch and immediately, she's out."

Dotty says she once caught Tammy nodding off during a game.

"I was sitting next to her, and I saw her jerk her head," Dotty said.

It was during a timeout, but still...

The 2004 season – his second at Ohio State – would come and go without Tank Whaley getting into a game. He had been moved to center, where height wasn't as much of an issue, but junior Nick Mangold was the starter and both Steve Winner and Doug Datish practiced as Mangold's backups.

It was not a good year for anyone buried on the depth chart to see playing time, anyway. The season was a struggle, with few blow-outs.

OSU would start out Big Ten play 0-3 before sophomore quarterback Troy Smith and freshman receiver Ted Ginn Jr. helped inject some life into the offense and salvage an 8-4 campaign which included a win over Michigan and an Alamo Bowl thumping of Oklahoma State.

Tank had been impressing coaches with his scout-team work since his first few weeks of practice the previous year. Now, other scout-team players started looking to him as an example, as well.

"Young guys coming in kind of listened to me, and I became kind of the captain of the scout team," he says.

Each week during the season, coach Jim Tressel hands out various awards: offensive and defensive players of the week, lineman of the week, the big hit of the week, and so on.

Usually he awards a scout team offensive, defensive and special teams player of the week, as well.

When he announces the scout-team awards at his Tuesday news conferences, most reporters politely put their pens down for a second. Space in the paper is at a premium, and frankly, not enough people care about players they've never heard of to make it worth printing.

But to the scout-teamers, of course, it's a big deal. Whaley won one of those awards in 2004.

The reason it's significant and not just a small line of type buried in a 20-page press release is because it means the head coach recognizes your ability. By this time, Tressel definitely had noticed the stocky bulldog from Ironton.

"He worked tremendously hard and he was so smart," Tressel says. "He picked up the center position, and that takes a whole lot of preparation. All of a sudden he kind of grew on everybody – through his enthusiasm and his passion, he became a leader on the team. Everybody loved Tank."

It was another morale boost. And it quickly became the next in his series of small goals he set – to win the award every week.

"I loved that," he said. "It's recognition for people who don't get recognition on Saturday. At that point, I'm not thinking I'm going to play, so that was the big thing for me."

Tank was pass-blocking in practice the week before the Wisconsin game when somebody fell on the outside of his right ankle. He knew he was hurt, but he went to the sideline, got taped up, and went back in.

"But I could hardly push off it," he said. "I tried and tried, but it was worthless. (The defender) would just roll me back and throw me down. I could hardly get off the ball, let alone get to where I needed to be."

If Whaley couldn't be in the proper position to simulate where a Badgers blocker was going to be on Saturday, he was not helping the team by trying to gut it out. So he was done for the day.

Later, the training staff took a look and diagnosed a severe high ankle sprain. You're out two to four weeks, they said.

Whaley just about broke into a cold sweat.

"I can't sit out four weeks," he thought. "I don't have that kind of time. I'm a walk-on, I don't have any cushion."

His fear was that he could be easily replaced, and by the time he healed, he'd be forgotten.

"As a walk-on, they don't have you on a contract, saying they'll pay for your school," he says. "That's the way I always thought about it."

Ohio State lost to Wisconsin, its second straight loss, and was headed to Iowa the following week.

Whaley went to trainers Doug Calland and Bob Sweeney and

proclaimed himself ready for that week's practice.

"Prove it," they said. "Run on it."

"All right," Tank said, "what do you want me to do?"

Jog around the field twice.

"I remember thinking, 'Oh my gosh,'" Whaley recalls.

He had the ankle taped up so tightly it was practically cutting off the circulation. He told himself he couldn't limp, as the trainers would be watching him closely.

"I gritted my teeth the whole way around, but I did it," he said.

Sweeney and Calland shook their heads and grudgingly approved his return to practice.

"They said, 'Only you, only an Ironton guy, would be able to come out and do that,'" Whaley says.

All week he suffered. Every time the ankle was bumped, it hurt. For about two weeks, Whaley was in pain before it started healing.

All this, just so he could practice – just to do his part to make other players better, with no personal glory at stake. He was driven only by his inner pride and work ethic.

During these first few years at OSU, whenever Tammy would call her son, she always asked him the same question: "Is it worth it?"

Yeah, mom, he'd answer.

"He got tired of hearing it, but I had to hear him say it was worth it," she says.

Tank wasn't lying. Of course he wanted to play, but he was one of those few players who really was just happy to be there.

Even though he got constant atta-boys for his scout-team work – and won that award for it – the ray of light Whaley had seen in his meeting with Bollman the previous winter had started to fade.

Two years had elapsed, and he couldn't see that he was any closer to seeing the field.

"That was a time when I was like, 'Man, you know, I might do this the rest of my career,'" Whaley says. "You've just got to kind of accept it, sit down with yourself and say, 'I'm just glad I'm here.'

"That's how it was. I walked on, I didn't expect anything. I kind of made up my mind that I'm here to stay, and if I play scout team for five years and that's what I need to do for the team, than that's what I'm going to do."

CHAPTER 8:

Breakthrough

By the beginning of 2005, the Ohio State coaching staff had fallen in love. If only every player practiced as hard and cared as much about maximizing his talent as Tank Whaley did.

But as much as he was a scout-team demon, the staff didn't see how Whaley was going to play much at center with Nick Mangold at that spot. Now a senior, Mangold was a top contender for the Rimington Award, given to the nation's best center.

The Buckeyes also were bringing in Jim Cordle, a highly regarded freshman who was Mangold's likely heir apparent.

Unlike 2004, though, this OSU team was expected to be dominating. With Troy Smith and Ted Ginn returning on offense and linebacker A.J. Hawk somewhat surprisingly coming back for his senior year, maybe the Buckeyes would be comfortably ahead enough to sneak Whaley into a few games.

So, just like in the previous year, the first hint of things to come came from offensive line coach Jim Bollman in those offseason one-on-one meetings.

In the 2004 meeting, Bollman had put the kibosh on Whaley's long snapping. This time, Bollman mentioned a magic word: scholarship.

Actually, three magic words: Scholarship, and playing time.

"He told me if I kept working hard, he was going to try to start working on getting me out there (on the field)," Tank said.

That encouragement continued through spring practice. Bollman told him he was practicing well.

As spring practice came to a close, defensive coordinator Mark Snyder was hired as head coach at Marshall, his alma mater.

As an Ironton native, Snyder had been the link that brought Whaley to Ohio State. On the urging of his old high school coaches,

Snyder was basically Whaley's sponsor, for lack of a better term.

When Snyder left, OSU coach Jim Tressel worried that he might offer Whaley a scholarship to go with him.

"I was nervous," Tressel said. "I thought (Whaley) was such a great part of the program, and maybe he would go with Mark and help him make the transition and help build the Marshall program.

"I never said a word to Mark or to Tank, but deep down I was hoping Mark wouldn't take him. I loved having (Whaley) here."

Snyder did not make that offer and Whaley stayed. And when Tank reads this, he probably will be shocked to learn how much concern his potential departure had caused Tressel.

So the coaching staff continued to whisper sweet nothings into Whaley's ears. That was nice, but they weren't paying the bills.

Tank's family was heading into its third year of trying to put him through school. Even with Tammy's bakery business doing well, funds were beginning to run short.

The days of heading home to traditional summer jobs are long gone for Division I football players. Players are "encouraged" to stick around for summer workouts, which are about as optional as breathing, if you want to play.

Tressel has said there are only about five weeks a year when the Buckeyes are not doing some sort of football-related activities, such as lifting, conditioning, informal workouts or whatever.

The two weeks after a bowl game are off, as mandated by the NCAA. Besides that break, there's one week in spring, one week just before the start of preseason camp and a week around Christmas.

That's about it. At OSU, football is a 47-week job.

Staying on campus for the summer is relatively easy for scholarship players. If they are enrolled in summer school, their room-and-board stipends keep rolling in. Walk-ons, though, arguably have more at stake in terms of proving themselves over the summer, yet they have no readily available source of income.

Whaley had stuck around Columbus in the summer of 2004 and planned to do so again in 2005. This time, though, he went looking for a job. He wanted to take some of the pressure off his mother.

One of his fellow walk-ons had heard there were openings on the Ohio Stadium maintenance crew, and before long, Tank was working there.

The duties were varied and menial: painting the walls of the concession stands, painting trash cans, whatever needed done.

He worked eight hours a day for seven bucks an hour. At the same time, his pride paid a price.

At times, he would look around the stadium and laugh ruefully to himself.

"I'm like, 'I'm on this football team, but I have yet to see the field,'" he said. "I guess this was my way of seeing the field."

Nobody wishes injury on a teammate, but the reality is that Tank Whaley caught a break just after fall camp opened in August 2005. Jim Cordle, his toughest competition to back up Mangold at center, had enrolled in time for spring ball and impressed the coaches.

That probably meant Whaley was ticketed for third-string duties again. But in the first few days of practice, Cordle broke a bone in his foot. He would end up being redshirted.

And that opened the door to the possibility of playing time.

Still, Whaley had no hint of what was to come when sixth-ranked Ohio State met Miami of Ohio in the first game that fall, on September 3. Even with Troy Smith serving an NCAA suspension and quarterback Justin Zwick starting, the Buckeyes cruised.

Zwick threw a touchdown pass. Antonio Pittman rushed for 100 yards. When third string quarterback Todd Boeckman threw a TD to Ted Ginn late in the third quarter, it was 34-0.

In the waning minutes of the game, the call came: Whaley, get in there. Two years earlier, Tank had been watching the OSU opener from a seat in the stands.

Now he made his collegiate debut.

"It was like one of those out-of-body kinds of things," he said. "Like, 'I finally made it.'"

It was strictly mop-up duty, nothing to write home about. Except that immediately afterward, home wrote him. He turned on his cell phone to discover he had about a dozen text messages, mostly from back in Ironton.

He was one of theirs. A fighting Tiger.

"People were like, 'Man, I saw you on TV,'" Whaley recalls. "That was pretty neat. A lot of people don't get that. For (Ironton residents) to know somebody playing for Ohio State, it makes them feel like they were part of it.

"It's always gratifying to know you mean that much to other people, and that people out there care about you.

"I was like, 'OK, this is why you come here and work here.'"

Even that, though, wasn't his fondest memory of the game. That came just after he dressed and walked out of the locker room to greet his beaming mother.

"Do you realize you just played in a game?" Tammy said.

They both knew how much had gone into that moment. Arm in arm, they went out to celebrate over a nice meal.

One family member who was not there to share his break-through game was his grandmother, Dotty Tipton. She was battling cancer for the third time in six years.

In 1999, she had colon cancer. The following year, it was discovered in her liver. Two cycles of chemotherapy cleared those up.

But in 2005, Tank's third season, cancer was discovered in her lung. Thankfully it wasn't lung cancer, which is usually fatal, but a remnant of her earlier cancer that had reappeared.

She had surgery to remove a section of her lung and underwent chemotherapy again.

"That last time was the worst," Dotty says.

The drug she was taking had strange and severe effects, one of which was an aversion to anything cold. She couldn't pick up ice cubes.

She definitely couldn't be outside in typical Ohio fall weather, so she watched Tank's games on television. It was difficult – she and Tommy had helped raise Tank from infancy and were like parents to him.

But she had no choice.

"He would call me before every game and tell me, 'Mamaw, I'll be thinking of you,'" Dotty says.

"She never once complained, she's the strongest woman I know on the face of the earth," says Missy Leonard, Dotty's daughter and Tank's aunt. "She'd even cook for us when she was sick. We were like, 'We need to be cooking for you.' She's our pillar of strength."

To a point. After enduring the first treatment of that brutal chemo regimen, she asked the doctors if she could skip the final two treatments. They grudgingly agreed.

Despite that, Dotty has remained cancer free since then.

Playing in his first game did not relieve Tank of scout-team duties. Far from it. He was Captain Scout Team, fast approaching legendary status.

If Ohio State ever forms a Scout Team Hall of Fame, he would be a charter member.

In fact, Whaley made it a point of pride not to miss a play all season. Jim Tressel estimates the team runs about 200 plays a week. Multiply that by 12 game weeks, plus bowl practice, and the number of plays in a season probably approaches 3,000.

Tressel marveled at Tank's dedication to such a thankless task.

"He would never come out unless you made him," Tressel says. "He wanted to do the best he could. I have great respect for him."

Whaley added two more scout team player of the week awards to the one he garnered in 2004.

His attitude had changed ever so slightly, though. When he was a scared redshirt freshman in 2003, he had simply accepted the innumerable small frustrations that come with being a glorified tackling dummy.

By now, he had a taste of playing time and a hunger for more. Everyone looked up to him on the practice field. He was well established, and on one memorable day, he allowed anger to briefly take over.

Practice jerseys are the worst. They're loose, rather than the state-of-the-art, form-fitting shirts worn on game days.

That makes linemen particularly susceptible to being grabbed by the jersey and yanked around. Whaley's neck was constantly rubbed raw from this.

"One day, they ripped it so hard it ripped the jersey half off of me," Tank says. "I was just fed up with it."

In his best Incredible Hulk impression, he let out a roar and ripped the rest of his jersey off. He threw the torn shirt to the ground and prepared for the next play wearing bare shoulder pads.

Defensive coordinator Jim Heacock took notice. Mild mannered off the field, Heacock turns into an alpha male between the lines. His competitive heart loved that scene with Tank.

"Yeah, that's what I'm talking about!" he hollered to the team. "Might as well take off your helmet, too, and play with no pads."

Tank probably would have done that, had he been asked.

Ohio State's national-title aspirations had died with two losses in its first five games (to Texas and Penn State). But once Troy Smith returned from suspension and got his feet under him again, the Buckeyes cruised.

They won a key come-from-behind game against Michigan State to improve to 4-2 and then just started crushing Big Ten opponents: 41-10 over Indiana, 45-31 at Minnesota, 40-2 against Illinois and 48-7 against Northwestern.

With scores like that, Whaley got more mop-up duty. His best stretch was playing six minutes against Illinois and five minutes the next week against Northwestern.

As it turns out, the best thing that happened to Tank Whaley that season wasn't on the field, but occurred after that Northwestern game, on November 12.

He and his roommates hosted a 1980s-themed party that night. Among the guests was Brittany Benjamin.

Brittany was from Hurricane, West Virginia, a town of about 5,000 located halfway between Huntington and Charleston. It's on a major interstate (I-64) and near enough to both cities that it's not a down-in-the-holler type of place.

It's also not too far from Ironton – maybe 45 miles.

She had some Ohio roots. Her father, Brad, was a graduate of Upper Arlington High School, in the shadow of Ohio Stadium, and Brittany grew up a Buckeyes fan.

Her passion was dance. She was on her high-school dance team (the type that performs at halftime of basketball games, for example), and her choice of colleges was dictated by whether or not she was accepted onto their dance teams.

She was accepted by Clemson and Ohio State, which made her choice an easy one.

On that fateful November 2005 day, Brittany actually was dragged to the party at Tank's place.

"I'm not big on parties, I can take them or leave them," she says. "I figured I'd go with my friends and tough it out until they were ready to leave."

She was talking with friends when she noticed a guy across the room. It was hard not to notice Tank that night. He had gone all-out for the 80s look: washed-out, tight-fitting jeans, a blue Superman T-shirt, a Bruce Springsteen-style headband and huge, white Nike tennis shoes.

He was air-guitaring and lip-synching to "Rock You Like a Hurricane," by the Scorpions.

"And he was pointing at me and staring at me, like he was singing it to me," Brittany said.

Equally amused and horrified, she left the room. A mutual friend tracked her down, though, and introduced the two.

They talked, and every few minutes she asked Tank if he knew her name. It was her own little test of a man's mindset. He kept answering correctly, seven or eight times in all. And then he asked if he could call her sometime.

Finally convinced this guy was OK, Brittany gave him her cell number, said goodnight, and went to find her friends.

Before she left, her phone rang. It was Tank. That was his own little test, to make sure she hadn't given him a fake number.

Despite that mutually mistrustful start, Brittany says she immediately knew he was the one. They spoke the next day, went on a date by the end of the week, and have been inseparable ever since.

He also has been entertaining her ever since.

"When I have the worst day ever and I'm just so down, he can say one thing and turn my day rightside up," Brittany says. "He makes me laugh like no other person can. We'll be in the grocery store, and I'll be going down the aisle, and he'll come down the aisle toward me and start dancing or moonwalking. I'm embarrassed, but it's so funny.

"And he's so loving and thoughtful and compassionate. He remembers things most guys forget about. He remembers what I wore on our first date."

Tank Whaley's totals that season, then, add up like so: six (games played), 19 (minutes of playing time) ... and one (soulmate).

Playing in a few games didn't help his checkbook, so Tank went back to work on the stadium maintenance crew in the summer of 2006.

By now, he was bonding with his fellow workers. They knew he played football, obviously, but he wasn't the type of guy who held that over any of them. He wasn't a big-timer.

He sweated with them, and on one scary day in July, he bled with them.

Among the crew's many duties was setting up the stadium for the season. With camp fast approaching, Whaley and his colleagues were putting up the goalposts. They are stored underneath the south stands in the offseason.

While pushing the heavy posts out of storage, the wheels caught on a crease in the concrete. Whaley's momentum caused him to stumble forward and fell into the post.

He happened to hit it right where the bolts that secure the posts into the ground were sticking out. His left leg was deeply gashed.

It required a trip to the hospital, a tetanus shot and 12 stitches.

At this point, with Mangold graduated, Whaley appeared to be the solid No. 2 center behind Doug Datish, a two-year starter who was being moved from guard for his senior season.

Leaving the hospital, all Whaley could think of was, "Great, I'm finally getting to play, and now I won't be ready for camp."

He was ready, barely. The stitches came out two days before practice began. Running gassers on the first day was a painful experience, but he managed. Ironically, that was the worst injury he suffered at Ohio State.

It was right about that time that Whaley earned his first raise in two summers. He went from $7 an hour to $7.25.

Anybody who has seen the movie *The Jerk* can imagine how Tank might have been as excited when the 2006 media guide came out as Steve Martin's character was at being in the phone book.

In the 2003 media guide, he wasn't mentioned at all. In 2004 and 2005, his presence on the team was marked by a single line on the roster.

It had taken four years, but finally Whaley's picture and a biography were included. Maybe someone was trying to fore-shadow what was to come.

In most of Tressel's seven seasons, as camp draws to a close, a few walk-ons get put on scholarship. This has not been strictly out of charity, mind you – Tressel would rather have his roster full of five-star recruits.

But when one of those prospects spurns OSU on signing day, or when players transfer or leave unexpectedly for any reason, Tressel often rewards hard-working walk-ons rather than bank the extra scholarships for the following signing day.

Headed into the team meeting where this would be announced, Whaley was hopeful, but realistic. There were at least two deserving seniors that he figured would be in line to get a scholarship before he would: running back Ryan Franzinger and receiver Derek Harden.

And he had no idea how many scholarships would be handed out. Two might be it.

"I thought, 'They're probably not going to give it to me this year,'" he said.

Indeed, Franzinger and Harden were announced. Tank felt his heart leap, though, when a third scholarship was awarded, to fullback Trever Robinson. Like him, Robinson was a fourth-year junior.

Would they award a fourth? They would, and it went to Tank Whaley.

For Tank, it was more than a relief from the financial strain. It was sweet validation, an acknowledgement that yes, he was indeed good enough to be awarded a football scholarship to Ohio State, and they don't hand those out like candy, either.

As usual, his first thought wasn't for himself, but for his mother. When the meeting broke up, he went to his car and called his mother.

"I started screaming," Tammy says. "Oh my gosh, it just hit me emotionally. The greatest thing had happened – he had earned something. A lot of people are given scholarships right out of high school, bot they hadn't earned something like Tyler. They had been given something for playing against high-school kids."

Tank's recollection of that phone call: "She went from the screaming stage to the crying stage and back to the screaming stage."

His next call was to Brittany, who furthered his hearing loss.

"I started screaming," she said. "I went out and bought balloons and (candy) Buckeyes and brought them in to him. It had bothered me since we started dating, how hard he worked and he wasn't getting the recognition."

Something about this scholarship thing brings out the vocal side of his family and friends, apparently. A few weeks later, during a break in one of the Buckeyes' home games, the new scholarship players were announced to the crowd in Ohio Stadium.

Chad Parker, Whaley's former Ironton High teammate, stood

up and started cheering like a wild man.

"Everybody was looking at me like I was crazy," Parker says. "I was one of the only people in the stands who knew who he was."

As the season was about to begin, Brittany left him.

No, not in that way. She was headed to the University of Cincinnati for the final year-and-a-half of her schooling.

She came to OSU planning to major in nursing, but halfway through that first year, after volunteering at a hospital, she decided it wasn't for her.

The following spring, both of her grandfathers passed away. At one of their funerals, she got to talking to the funeral-home director and decided she might want to go into that field, instead.

"It still had some aspect of nursing, because you're still helping families," Brittany says.

Ohio State doesn't have a mortuary science program; Cincinnati does. So she bid a temporary farewell to Tank, although the two would wear a groove in I-71 over the next 15 months, traveling back and forth to see each other.

And as it turned out, many more people than just Brittany saw Tank Whaley that September.

Ever since Texas had dashed the Buckeyes' 2005 title hopes with an epic victory in Ohio Stadium, OSU looked forward to evening the score in Austin the next fall.

Vince Young was gone from the defending national champion Longhorns. Troy Smith was still around, so OSU felt pretty good about its chances. The Buckeyes were ranked No. 1, Texas No. 2.

One of OSU's big concerns, though, was handling the Texas heat. Not the pass rush – the temperature. Game time was 7 p.m. locally, but this was September 9 in the South, and Austin was coming off a record-setting August heat wave. The thermometer was likely to be in the high 80s with heavy humidity at game time.

The Buckeyes experimented with space-age cooling suits on their sideline. But Tressel planned to combat the weather with an old-fashioned approach, as well – substitute freely.

The atmosphere was idyllic in Austin that evening, what college football is all about. Fans streamed toward the bright stadium lights in the growing dusk, a healthy chunk of scarlet peppering the burnt-orange, cowboy-hat-wearing flood.

The Buckeyes moved the ball well on their two opening drives but had nothing to show for it.

Texas marched down and looked ready to open the scoring when a little-known sophomore linebacker named James Laurinaitis knocked the ball out of Billy Pittman's grasp at the OSU 2-yard line.

Donald Washington recovered for the Buckeyes and raced up the sideline before being knocked out of bounds at the 50.

OSU had been subbing in already on defense, but Tressel had been waiting for the right moment to do it offensively. This was it, in good field position and with momentum.

In trotted the entire second-team offensive line, which was, from left to right: Steve Rehring, Kyle Mitchum, Tank Whaley, Ben Person and Jon Skinner.

In 2006, Whaley (54) had the privilege of snapping to Heisman Trophy-winning quarterback Troy Smith (10). Here, he prepares for a play against Cincinnati. (Photo by Scott Terna)

This took guts.

"That was interesting," starting right tackle Kirk Barton said. "We had never done that before – put in the (backups) on the third drive. I was like, 'Are you serious?' But it ended up paying off."

On the first play, Smith rolled out and found Anthony Gonzalez for 26 yards. He then threw incomplete. Next, Mitchum was called for a false start. Smith zipped an out pass to Gonzalez for 17 yards and a first down at the Texas 12.

A Smith draw failed, but on the next snap, he rolled out and hit Gonzalez in the front right corner of the end zone for a touchdown.

The drive consisted of five plays, 50 yards and took just 1 minute, 22 seconds off the clock. OSU would never trail and would go on to post a convincing 24-7 victory that would cement the Buckeyes' status as the team to beat nationally.

After the players sang "Carmen Ohio" to the contingent of Buckeyes fans in the corner of Darrell K. Royal Stadium, Gonzalez – the epitome of unselfishness – made a point of saying how happy he was that a guy like Tank Whaley was a part of such an important drive in such a momentous game.

Watching on television like the rest of the nation, Brittany "went hysterical," she said. "I was screaming."

Finally, everything seemed to be falling into place for Whaley. He was the solid No. 2 center for the top-ranked college football team, playing a few minutes each game.

At times, he was snapping the ball to a future Heisman Trophy winner. Who would have guessed that, three years earlier?

He had been put on scholarship, easing his family's financial worries. He had a beautiful girlfriend.

Life was good. For the moment, at least. Tank Whaley's OSU career had rarely been without struggles, and now more were just around the corner.

After sitting out 2005 with a broken foot, Jimmy Cordle now was healthy. And it started becoming apparent that despite Whaley forcing his way into the mix, the coaching staff still considered Cordle the center of the future.

In week 6 and 7, Cordle got the mop-up minutes at center and Whaley didn't play. In fact, after the fourth week of the season, Whaley played in only two games, and that came only after Cordle played extensive minutes first.

Suddenly, after a year and a half as the top backup, Tank had been pushed back down to third string.

Logically he understood. Cordle was 6-4, 285 and a heralded recruit. He had three years of eligibility left after this season, Whaley had one. It made sense, but that didn't make him feel better about it.

"I knew that was who, in their eyes, was going to be the next (center), so it's only logical you've got to get this guy some playing time," Tank said. "But you always want to be the best, and then just to get kind of put aside... I'm thinking, 'Wow, he's outperformed me in practice, or they think he's better than me, that's always hard to swallow.'"

In reality, his grandfather's old fears about Tank falling victim to politics seemed to be coming true. When the push came, the undersized walk-on would get shoved aside.

"I understand that, but at the same time I didn't want to accept it," Whaley said. "I wanted to be that guy. You've got to have the realistic view, but at the same time, you have to be dreamy."

His final numbers for 2006 were a bit ominous: He played in six games, the same as 2005. But he played just 16 minutes, three fewer than the previous season. It was not an upward trend any longer.

Back in Ironton, his parents had seen a photo on the Internet of Tank about to snap the ball to Troy Smith in a September game against Cincinnati. They tracked down the photographer and ordered hundreds of copies, which they gave to friends as Christmas presents.

They took one, sized it down, and made it into an ornament that hung on their Christmas tree that winter.

It was a moment to remember, obviously. But as Tank Whaley sat home that holiday, he might have looked at that photo with mixed feelings.

For the fourth straight year, he had not played against Michigan. He would not play in the national championship game, either.

With one season left in his Ohio State career, was that moment as good as it would get? Were his best days behind him?

CHAPTER 9:

"Can You Play Fullback?"

Three quest for "inside" information about Ohio State football is constant and intense. The Internet is full of message-board posters that claim to have connections, and they drop pearls of wisdom – who's looking good in practice, who's not – to an eager hoard of lurkers.

It wouldn't surprise me if Buckeye players themselves search the Internet for information, because there are many times when it seems they are the last to know what's going on, even when it deals with their own career.

In the preseason of 2004, when Troy Smith and Justin Zwick were competing fiercely for the starting quarterback position, Jim Tressel one day nonchalantly announced that Zwick would start the opening game.

When the quarterbacks met the media a few minutes later, it was clear that Smith had not yet been informed of that decision.

So it probably shouldn't be a surprise that Tank Whaley first heard rumblings that he might move to fullback from Eric Lichter, the team's strength and conditioning coach.

Lichter had attended a staff meeting where the coaches were discussing a need to find more fullbacks. With Smith gone and rising sophomore Beanie Wells on hand, the plan for 2007 was to go back to more of a traditional power-oriented run game.

Senior Dionte Johnson and former walk-on Trever Robinson were the only fullbacks available, and the coaches were looking for one more.

Someone mentioned Tank. He knew the offense cold, having been a center for three seasons. He certainly had the body build for it. With some footwork practice, why not?

Whaley's first reaction was skepticism. I've actually played some at center, why move me?

Back home, this was also what his family thought at first: Oh no, he's worked so hard to get on the field, and now, after four years, they're shuffling him aside.

But by the time he had his annual meeting with offensive co-ordinator Jim Bollman, Whaley had begun to embrace the idea.

So when Bollman said they were thinking of trying him at fullback, Whaley answered evenly and confidently, "I think I can do it."

After all, for years, many of his friends, including several OSU players and football staff members, had suggested fullback might be a good spot for him.

His Ironton High buddy Chad Parker says, "I thought that right off the bat, that walking on at a Division I school, unless you were 6-6, 320 pounds, you're not going to play as a lineman. I knew Tank had good footwork and size, and I always told him he should try out at fullback when he had a chance."

Jim Walker, sports editor of the *Ironton Tribune*, says, "I told him a long time ago he would make a heckuva fullback. I thought they wasted him on the line."

Of course, this is hindsight, spoken after Whaley successfully made the conversion. When I told Tressel that many of Tank's friends thought he should have switched to fullback earlier, he laughed.

"I didn't get a lot of letters or e-mails from Ironton, telling me I had a dynamic fullback in the mix," he chuckled. "He wasn't the kind of guy who was going to walk in to my office and say, 'Here's what I should be playing.'"

Tressel knows Tank well, and he's exactly right about that. Whaley wishes now that he had played fullback earlier in his career, "because here I was, trying to play center at 5-11, 280."

But it's a lot easier to say that to yourself than to actually go knock on Tressel's door and suggest it.

"I never felt like I was in a position where I could go in like, 'Hey, I think I need to do this or that,' so I never did," he says.

Around that time, Tressel bumped into Whaley in the hall-ways of the football facility.

"Can you play fullback?" Tressel asked.

"Yeah, coach."

"Are you going to lose 10 pounds?" Tressel said.

"Yeah, I can lose that."

And Tressel, who likes to keep his players on edge – the better to make them focus on improvement – answered, "I guess we're going to find out."

It didn't take long for Tank to find out why losing those 10 pounds was so important. He realized it on the second day of the team's 6 a.m. winter conditioning drills.

He didn't realize it the first day because he spent that session working with the offensive line. Nobody had officially told him he was switching, or when the switch took effect.

Adding to his confusion, Bollman had told him they did not want him to completely forget about being a center. Though Connor Smith was second to Cordle on the depth chart, Smith was coming off a redshirt season and had never played.

So Tank would provide valuable experience and might even start if Cordle got hurt.

Therefore, Whaley had no idea what to do that first day of workouts. He was not one to make waves or speak up, so he just did what he had done for the previous four years.

"At the end, (Bollman) came over to me (and said), 'Man, I messed up today, you need to work with the running backs tomorrow,'" Whaley says. "So that was it. They were switching me, and the second day, I was with the fullbacks, and I was one ever since."

It was on that second day that Whaley felt the full weight of his 282-pound body.

After 48 minutes of drill work in their respective positions, the Buckeyes finish their early-morning workouts with a team session. Tressel runs that part personally. The idea is to do something that builds camaraderie – or causes you to pass out, one or the other.

One of the staples of that session is called a "snake drill."

That consists of backpedaling across the field, shuffling sideways, sprinting forward, shuffling over, backpedaling, and repeating until you eventually make your way back across the field.

The big boys on the offensive and defensive lines are told to shuffle and sprint at 10-yard intervals. The skill position players have to shuffle, sprint and cut every 5 yards.

So that doubles the amount of cutting. It was absolute torture for a guy like Tank, who had a lineman's body but now was lumped in with the small guys.

"It's a world of difference," offensive tackle Kirk Barton says. "And all of a sudden, Tank is running with kids like (speedy cornerback) Donald Washington. That was something, when I saw that.

"Offensive linemen, we're in decent shape, but we're not in defensive back shape. We're not meant to go long distances. And to see Tank with the body and frame of an offensive lineman... I would've died doing that, it looked hard."

It felt hard. That first day, Whaley was that proverbial guy who brings up the rear of the drill, so far behind that everyone else is done and clapping, encouraging him to finish.

"I just remember my legs being about ready to lock up, and I'm thinking in my head, 'This sucks.' And also that I've got to lose some weight, or I'm going to kill myself."

Whaley immediately changed his eating habits. Tops on the list was cutting out pizzas and wings, "all that good stuff," he says.

"And I was the guy who was like, competitive eating. I was going to Hooters and trying to eat 65 wings, trying to keep up with Boonie (offensive tackle Alex Boone) and them."

Boonie and them were his buddies – guys he had spent years with on the offensive line. Positions groups develop close relationships, like families within a family, and it was tough to leave that behind when Whaley switched.

Equally worrisome was how the fullbacks would react to another competitor being thrown into their midst. A guy like Dionte Johnson, entering his final season, was probably thrilled at the change in offensive styles back to the power game. It meant he would be dug out of mothballs and play again.

And suddenly, on the eve of camp, he has to contend with Tank? The chemistry was a cause for concern.

"Here I was, barging in, a senior, and I didn't want to feel like I was stepping on their toes," Whaley said. "But Dionte and Trev (Robinson), they really took me in, and that's what made the transition a lot easier. They helped me out, they never said, 'This guy could be competition, so I'm not going to help him.' They helped me with everything I possibly asked of them, and that made it a lot smoother."

Meanwhile, his diet was working. He reported to camp that fall 17 pounds lighter, at 265.

He reported lighter in spirit, too, thanks to an event that summer.

Despite getting the scholarship in August 2006, Whaley went back for a third year of working on the stadium maintenance crew in 2007.

That seemed unnecessary, except that Tank had been planning something for awhile, and he needed the key to the stadium that working there allowed him to have.

Since the previous summer, Tank and his girlfriend, Brittany Benjamin, had talked about marriage. In general, they decided they'd wait until they were out of college.

Brittany would occasionally leave pictures of engagement rings lying around Tank's apartment, but that was about the extent of it. No rush.

On the morning of Sunday, July 8, Whaley said he had a football meeting to attend and left. Brittany thought nothing of it.

Her family and his family were coming to town later that day to take a tour of the stadium. Though both families had of course sat in the stands for years, there is an official stadium tour that takes visitors behind the scenes and into areas normally off limits.

Tank came back home, gathered everyone, and off they went. They toured the band room, the press box and television booths, the luxury suites and the locker room. Brittany tried on Tank's football pads and got down in a three-point stance. Everyone was having fun.

Then it was time to see the actual field. Ohio State was just finishing up the process of installing prescription athletic turf. No matter what the surface, it's a real treat for anyone to stand on the floor of that massive structure and look around.

The grandparents and a few others stayed in the stands while Tank, Brittany and the rest of the family headed to field level. When they got to the edge of the turf, Tank grabbed Brittany's hand, and his pace quickened.

"I felt like I was sprinting, he was dragging me out there," Brittany recalls.

As they neared midfield, Tank started twisting off the ring Brittany wore, one her parents had given her.

"He said, 'I don't think you need that anymore,'" she says, "and by the time I could say, 'Why not?' he was down on a knee."

You know what comes next.

In July 2007, Tank proposed to Brittany Benjamin on the 50-yard line at Ohio Stadium. She said yes, of course. (Family photo)

Tank says that he said,"You've made me the happiest man ever. I love you so much. Will you be my wife?"

Brittany says, "I didn't hear half of what he said, I was zoned out."

Tank put the ring on her finger, kneeling dead-center in the Block O. Tank's younger sister, Madison, barely had time to snap pictures, it all happened so fast.

Everyone hollered their approval, and they all headed back up to club level, where Tank's mother presented a cake inscribed with "She said yes!"

That's where Whaley had been that morning – bringing in the cake and making other last-minute preparations.

Brittany said her knees shook for a week afterward. The daughter of an Upper Arlington native, she had grown up tailgating and attending games at Ohio Stadium and claims she dreamed of a proposal at midfield.

"I couldn't have asked for a better proposal," she says.

The wedding is set for December 6, 2008.

It was an unusual bunch of Ohio State players that convened for camp that August.

Most of the players expected to play key roles were juniors: Boone, quarterback Todd Boeckman, receiver Brian Robiskie, defensive end Vernon Gholston, linebackers James Laurinaitis and Marcus Freeman and cornerback Malcolm Jenkins, to name a few.

The senior class wasn't necessarily small, but it was oddly configured. The recruiting class of 2003 had melted away steadily over the years, through a combination of injuries, academic troubles and transfers.

The only remaining original scholarship member of that class was Barton.

There were a few "true" seniors, but they were hardly stars: Dionte Johnson and linebacker Larry Grant. Grant had transferred from junior college prior to 2006, so he wasn't an established leader.

The remaining seniors were either walk-ons or former walk-ons like Whaley and Trever Robinson.

This created an interesting leadership dynamic. Even Barton, the clear-cut star of the senior class, was not a highly regarded recruit out of high school, and he plays right tackle, hardly a glamor spot.

Boeckman was not your typical hot-shot quarterback, either. He's a small-town guy from St. Henry, Ohio, quiet and laid back.

The point is, there was a gritty, blue-collar identity to the group.

Add to that the fact that few thought Ohio State would rebound so quickly from its 2006 title-game run. The offensive firepower was all gone, and pundits rightfully expected the Buckeyes to take a year to recalibrate.

At the preseason Big Ten meetings, OSU was picked to finish third in the conference, behind Michigan – which returned its senior trio of tackle Jake Long, quarterback Chad Henne and running back Mike Hart – and Wisconsin, which had a fine 2006 under first-year coach Brett Bielema.

The third-place prediction fell on fertile ground. The walk-on-laden Buckeyes senior class was accustomed to slights and low expectations. They knew how to internalize it, then use it to their advantage.

"I came in (to OSU) hearing, 'You're not good enough, you're not fast enough,' just like this team did (in 2007)," Whaley said. "So I fit right into this team. I've been there, so I kind of knew how to handle it. So did all the other walk-ons, they were in the same position.

"You've got that (determination) and you translate that down to the younger guys, and it kind of spreads out. And before you know it, you've got a team that basically has an identity of scrappy, hard-nosed, do whatever it takes."

And of course, this was the perfect scenario for Whaley. He thrived in this environment, where he suddenly found himself a respected elder. It had taken five years, but now, instead of wondering if he could fit in at Ohio State, Ohio State had molded itself into a Tank Whaley-type team.

"This team was the exact identity of me," he said. "So I think I fit in well with this team, better than I had the previous four."

And it just so happened to be his senior year, which made it even more special – a marriage of the man and the moment, so to speak.

Said Tank, "I can't complain."

Good team chemistry helps, but a pudding-soft schedule isn't a bad thing, either, to help an inexperienced offense ease into the season.

Ohio State opened with Youngstown State – the first Division I-AA opponent in OSU history – and then Akron, which was almost shameful in its unwillingness to try anything downfield offensively.

Boeckman rallied the Buckeyes from a halftime deficit for an important confidence-building win at Washington in week three, and OSU opened the Big Ten season with a lopsided win over Northwestern.

The defense was outstanding, and the offense was slowly gaining confidence, despite a nagging ankle problem that was limiting Wells.

The big news for Tank Whaley, though, was that he was playing. And for the first time in five years, he was really, truly playing an important role, not just coming in for mop-up minutes with the second or third team.

After two years of using fullbacks for about five plays a game, the Buckeyes went back to a fair amount of I-formation looks. Fullbacks were on the field probably 30 to 40 percent of the time.

Whaley, now No. 42, was alternating series with Johnson, sort of like co-first teamers, and Robinson was the third man in.

Tank is not flashy, but he is a consistent, effective lead blocker. He has a unique style, bursting out of his three-point stance at the snap with one leg and one arm sort of kicking out to the side. It looks a bit like a sprinter coming out of the blocks, except without the blazing speed.

He goes straight through a gap, finds his linebacker or safety to block, and meets him squarely. He doesn't necessarily pancake guys, but if he finds them, they're out of the play.

Tressel believes Whaley's years as an offensive lineman made him a better fullback.

"He was excellent, because he knew what he was doing," Tressel says. "He got in his stance, and he could hear his (o-line) buddies grumbling up front, or if it was loud, he could see their hand signals.

"And then we always say the guy with the low pad wins, and Tank had an advantage there because his were lower. He worked hard in the weight room, he was very strong, and he was excellent."

Whaley had been taking the field with the Buckeyes since 2003, but in 2007, it meant more because he was finally an integral part of the team. Here, Whaley (42) and the team come out of the tunnel before a game. (Photo by Steve Davis)

He also was on several special teams, serving as part of the initial blocking wedge on kickoff returns and playing some on the punt team, as well.

That's how Tank got his first career "touch." Washington scored just before halftime and with three seconds left, squibbed the ensuing kickoff. Whaley scooped it up at the 32 and returned it to the 42 before being tackled.

No, he didn't ask for the ball as a souvenir – not his style. He was too busy soaking up this wonderful, legitimate playing time.

"I loved the transformation (to fullback), I never once really doubted like, 'Man, should I go back to the line or not?'" he said. "It got me on special teams, and I loved that. It gave me opportunities to play and do the things this team needs me to do."

He took one for the team in week five at Minnesota. Whaley was playing well: In my game notes – of course written long before I decided to write a book about him – I kept writing "Whaley" in the margins on sizable runs by Beanie Wells or Maurice Wells.

On an 8-yard Maurice Wells run early in the fourth quarter, Tank got popped hard and was momentarily woozy. The clock stopped, the trainers came in, and he wobbled off the field, arms draped over trainers on either side.

Brittany, still down at the University of Cincinnati finishing up her degree, was watching on television.

"I was freaking out," she said. "The camera would not go back on him so I could see how he was."

She called Tammy but couldn't get through. Finally, TV showed Whaley on the sidelines laughing, and Brittany calmed down.

If he had known what the television commentators had said about him earlier in the game, he might have laughed even harder.

While complimenting Whaley on a good block, the announcers, catching a close-up glimpse of Whaley's smaller but still ample belly, quipped, "Now THAT'S what a fullback should look like. No six-pack on that guy."

After the game, another relatively easy victory, Whaley found a text on his phone from a buddy.

"Dude, did you hear what they said? They just zoomed in on your gut," the message read.

Tank went home and watched it for himself. He taped all the games, "because here I am, playing now, and that was a big thing for me."

The trainers recommended Whaley sit out the next week at Purdue, to give his head time to fully clear.

That was a sensible suggestion, but Tank wasn't going to miss a game – not this year, not when he was finally an integral part of this team.

Deep down inside, he still had that walk-on mentality, that if he missed a game, he might somehow get pushed aside, forgotten about, replaced.

He and the trainers compromised: He would be limited to playing special teams at Purdue. But the very next week, practicing for Kent State, he was back and ready to play full time.

"I was playing every other series," he said, "and I didn't want to take a back seat. I didn't ever feel secure at Ohio State, like this job was mine. I always felt I had to fight for my job, even to the very end."

He adds that if everyone felt that way, there would be fewer injuries. Whaley says he knows of some established veterans who sit out a practice here or there with relatively minor maladies, knowing their spot is safe. Cumulatively, that can have an effect on a team, hurting its preparation.

Kent State coach Doug Martin created a stir that next week when he said he was going to rotate his backups freely in order not to get his starters hurt for the Mid-American Conference race.

This notion infuriated OSU defensive coordinator Jim Heacock. He didn't believe it. It insulted his sense of competition.

But Martin was true to his word, substituting for his starting quarterback in the second quarter and his starting running back in the third.

Not surprisingly, the Buckeyes rolled, 48-3. And later that night, thanks to several more of the serial upsets that marked the 2007 season, it was clear Ohio State was going to be ranked No. 1 again come Sunday night.

Now all they had to do was win their final five games, and they would get a chance to redeem themselves for that 41-14 embarrassment in the 2006 title game.

And that's when the Buckeyes started leaning on Beanie and the ground game. Facing a three-game stretch against old-fashioned, physical Big Ten defenses (Michigan State, Penn State and Wisconsin), OSU buttoned down into the I-formation and pounded Beanie.

In those three games, all victories, Beanie's stat lines were: 31 for 221 and a TD, 25 for 133, and 21 for 169 and three scores.

Whaley was a big part of those efforts. He played nine minutes against the Spartans, eight against Penn State and seven against Wisconsin, by far the most extended playing time he ever experienced.

Whaley was having so much fun, he even enjoyed insults from visiting fans. The Penn State game was nationally televised in front of a "white out" crowd in Happy Valley, the same atmosphere in which OSU had wilted in 2005.

When he had been a lineman, Tank had stood out because he so much smaller than the others. Now that he has grouped with the running backs, though, he stood out because of, well, that gut.

"At Penn State, someone said, 'Hey 42, you ever heard of situps?'" Whaley chuckles.

"I was like,'Oh my gosh,' but I loved that stuff. It kind of gets you cranked up."

He played cranked up that night. In a masterpiece 37-17 victory, Whaley at one point blocked All-American linebacker Dan Connor to the ground.

Watching at home, Tank's grandfather, Tommy Tipton, saw Whaley slap Connor on the foot as he walked past him. That was rare for Tank, to be demonstrative in any way.

So later, he asked his grandson what that was all about.

"Just letting him know I was there," Whaley replied.

Tank may have been late to the fullback party, but he caught up fast. As the season wore on, the Buckeyes lined him up more often as an H-back, set behind the tight end and maybe going in motion as a so-called "move blocker."

"He acquired the ability to read things on the run and go to moving targets," offensive coordinator Jim Bollman said. "He kept improving as the year went on."

Barton said, "I was happy that he finally found a niche. He was really great down at the goal line, he knocked some guys over."

He still had no carries or catches, though. He figured he probably wouldn't get a rush attempt – OSU fullbacks had one rush in the past three seasons – but he remained hopeful he might get a reception.

In practice, he showed good hands and felt he was worthy of being a legitimate outlet receiver for Boeckman.

"He told me, 'Mom, I've never dropped a ball in practice,'" Tammy said.

But back in spring, when discussing Whaley's move to fullback, Jim Tressel had said, "If Tyler is in the game at fullback, it's not for the passing game. Now we may trick them and send him in and be pass-protecting with him, but I don't know that we'll feature him as a receiver."

His chances were running out. OSU was heading into week 11, its final game before an impending showdown with Michigan in Ann Arbor with the Big Ten title and berth in the championship game on the line.

The only team in the way was Illinois.

CHAPTER 10:
Devastation and Celebration

On the morning of November 9, 2007, Tank Whaley began what would be a tumultuous, emotional 36-hour stretch with a pair of hospital visits.

The first visit was regularly scheduled. Ohio State players do a lot of community service, and Whaley was among a group of Buckeyes visiting the James Cancer Hospital.

The second visit, though, was wrenching. For the eighth time in his seven years, Brett Leonard – Tank's cousin – was undergoing a life-saving surgery.

Tank and Brett had a tight bond. They were the only men in their generation of the Tipton/Vogelsong clan. Tank had been Tommy and Dotty Tipton's first grandchild. After Tammy married Dave Vogelsong, Dave's daughter Whitney joined the group. A few years later, Madison was born to Dave and Tammy.

Then there was a 12-year gap before Missy Leonard, one of Tyler's three aunts, had a child.

"We were so excited when Missy got pregnant," Whaley said. "I was 16 and Madison was like 11 or 12, and we finally had another little one coming."

The little one came, and then almost left. Just two days old and still in the maternity ward, Brett turned blue and struggled to breathe.

"He started to crash," Missy says. "He was about ready to die."

Doctors discovered a heart murmur, and after further tests, found that Brett had been born with hypo-plastic left heart syndrome.

Put in English, Brett's heart basically does not have a working left ventricle. His right ventricle must pick up the slack, which of course is too much strain for one chamber to handle.

Tank has always been close to his young cousin, Brett Leonard, who was born with a heart defect. Here the two of them spend time in Ohio Stadium during the team photo day in August 2005. (Family photo)

Missy and her husband were given three choices: Do nothing and their son would die; wait for a heart transplant, which was unlikely because of the rarity of available newborn hearts; or undergo a three-surgery procedure over the next two years to try and buy time.

What kind of choice was that? When Brett was five days old, doctors split open his chest for the first of three open-heart surgeries he would endure in his first two years.

After the third procedure, he suffered a stroke that left him blind for 12 days. Nine months after that, he developed an abscess on his brain that required surgery and caused mild brain damage.

With constant therapy and the tremendous love of his family, Brett has managed to develop into an energetic and happy kid. Tank has taken an active role in Brett's life, reading to him and playing Santa Claus at Christmas, among other things.

On the eve of the Illinois game, Brett was at Children's Hospital in Columbus to get a pacemaker inserted. His heart rate was starting to slow dangerously.

Tank got to the hospital, hoping to catch Brett before the surgery, but was too late. He sat with his aunt and grandparents as long as he could. Brett was still under the knife when Whaley left to head to pre-game meetings.

"Four hours later, after meetings, I called to see how he was, and he was still in surgery," Tank said.

It was an eight-hour affair. And all of these procedures are designed to buy time until he hopefully can get a heart transplant.

"It can never be fixed," Missy says. "They tell us the oldest living person born with this condition is 24. Their hearts just wear out quicker."

Brett, says Missy, "is our fighter."

He's only the latest in Whaley's long line of tough family members – the line that traces back to the teamster Spike Tipton, to the World War II vet Tom Tipton, to his cancer-surviving uncle Andy Whaley and three-time cancer survivor, grandmother Dotty Tipton.

Tank always had a balanced perspective on life, but his family's health struggles have sharpened it further.

"When you see people close to you struggle, you remember that when you want to complain," he says. "I'm not getting a scholarship or I'm getting beat on, but those people are having a lot, lot worse time."

Amazingly, Brett was discharged the next day. Missy said they got home in time to watch the Illinois game on TV.

Just about everyone else in Tank's family was in the Ohio Stadium stands for Senior Day. For Whaley, the emotions started swelling even before he ran out of the tunnel that day.

He recalls greeting his parents that morning at the team hotel, and the last skull session in St. John Arena – with the band blaring and the fans' outpouring of passion. Then came the walk into the stadium and dressing in the locker room.

And then, the tradition of each senior being introduced and running across the field to greet first coach Tressel, and then his parents.

Whaley said he experienced an odd mix of feelings that day.

"You're trying to hold it in, because deep down inside, you know you have to get ready to play a football game," he said. "But you also start thinking back to all the times in the past, and trying to take it all in."

Whaley's name was called, and he threw both arms in the air as he jogged onto the field. Five years of home games that started

The November 10, 2007 game against Illinois was Senior Day, the seniors' last game in Ohio Stadium. Whaley (42) has just heard his name called as he runs onto the field. (Family photo)

with him in street clothes, watching from the stands, was coming to an end.

"It was a moment of satisfaction," he said.

He greeted Tressel and ran over to Tammy, who of course was in tears. His father Rich and stepfather Dave Vogelsong, whom he calls his "other father," were out there, as well.

"That was all so emotional," Tank said. "Then you have to try and recover. They had the flyover, and then you get ready to rock."

By this time, Whaley was fully aware that each Saturday, he was playing for more than himself. He realized he was representing Ironton, giving his hometown something to point to with pride.

He was playing for his family, people like his uncle Andy Whaley, a die-hard Buckeyes fan.

"It was great to live vicariously through him," Andy says. "That's why I went to Ohio State, to get football tickets. And then to see him play, I don't have words for it."

And in a sense, Tank was playing for all of those who wished they could. Not only was he a walk-on, but he was a regular guy, someone people related to easily.

During games throughout that 2007 season, Whaley says he got a kick out of seeing some of his colleagues from his stadium maintenance job. Several of them were on the net crew, in charge of raising and lowering the nets behind the goalposts before and after place kicks.

They would see Tank and yell at him. He would pat his chest in acknowledgement.

"They took pride in the fact that I was one of them," Whaley says. "I wasn't just a football guy, they knew me from working together. I was representing them. They felt a part of it. They knew my story, that I had to work hard to make ends meet, and I wasn't someone who put himself on a pedestal. They could watch me play and say, 'He did what I did all summer.'"

They wanted him to chest-bump them as he ran onto the field, but he politely drew the line at that.

Whaley may have been ready to rock that day, as he said, but the Buckeyes as a whole certainly were not.

Illinois came in unranked but resurgent, a developing feel-good story in the Big Ten. Coach Ron Zook had endured records of 2-9 and 2-10 in his first two seasons, which included a 40-2 embarrassment in 2005 at Ohio Stadium.

But the Illini had a young playmaking quarterback named Juice Williams, and as a freshman in 2006, Williams had helped his team play top-ranked Ohio State down to the final seconds in Champaign, Illinois.

Now Illinois was 7-3 and full of confidence.

They also had a great game plan and played just about the perfect game. Running the shotgun spread option attack that had given OSU fits in the 2006 title game, Williams was masterful. His play-action passes caught the Buckeyes off guard, and he ended up throwing for four touchdowns despite coming into the game with just eight TDs in 10 games.

Ohio State curiously played on its heels defensively, and quarterback Todd Boeckman threw three interceptions.

The Buckeyes' dream season was in trouble, but in the midst of that stress came a memorable moment.

On first down from the Illinois 41-yard line, Boeckman looked downfield, found no receiver, and checked down. He tossed the ball to Whaley – his first career offensive touch.

In the stands, Tammy was stunned.

"I looked at Dave, and then I screamed, 'Run, Tyler, run!,'" she said.

Whaley looked like he was more conditioned to hit someone than to run to daylight. He went down after a 4-yard gain. It wasn't much, but it meant something to a former third-string walk-on center.

The game, though, came down to Williams in the fourth quarter with his team ahead 28-21 and trying to burn some clock.

Williams converted a fourth-and-inches, then four more third downs – all with quarterback keepers – as the Illini held the ball for the final 8:09 to pull off the shocking upset.

Tempers flared as several players pushed and shoved and threw a few punches at the midfield logo afterward.

Then the Buckeyes retreated to the locker room and tried to reconcile the fact that they had blown their chance to return to the national championship game. The loss would drop them from No. 1 to No. 7 in the bowl championship series standings.

With only three more weeks in the college football season, it was far-fetched to think that five teams ranked ahead of OSU would lose.

"It was bad after the game," Whaley said. "I teared up in the locker room. Nobody wants to lose their last game in the stadium. It was heartbreaking."

Still, he had all those family members out there waiting to go out to eat with him – people who had played such a big part in his going to Ohio State to begin with.

He couldn't mope for too long.

"Believe me, my emotions were well spent at the end of the game," he said. "But my family was there to support me, and it had been a good year, so I was not going to ruin the moment I had with them. They wanted to celebrate Senior Day, so I tried to hold my emotions in."

Almost immediately after the game, he had been pulled aside for an interview with the Ohio State radio network. Although at the time, he felt miserable and did not want to talk, the questioning turned toward the next game.

Talking and thinking about Michigan actually helped Tank refocus. In four years, he had never played in the Ohio State-Michigan game. In a week, he would.

"At least (Illinois) wasn't our last, last game," he said. "We had the Michigan game to redeem ourselves. I kept thinking that

I was finally going to get a chance to hit one of those guys wearing those stupid helmets."

If there's one thing above all else that Jim Tressel has brought back to the Ohio State football program, it's the emphasis on the tradition and mystique of the Michigan rivalry and the sense of pride in winning that game.

John Cooper was a fine football coach. His cardinal sin in 13 years at OSU, though, was not necessarily that he didn't win enough of the rivalry games, but that he never seemed to embrace its spirit, its down-deep-in-your-soul importance to the people of Ohio.

In contrast, from the day he was hired, Tressel – an Ohio native who fondly remembers watching "The Game" with his dad, Lee – has immersed his players completely in its history and urgency.

And that helps explain why, on the night before OSU met Michigan last November, lying awake in the team hotel, the magnitude of what he was about to do sunk in for Tank Whaley.

"This is what Ohio State is all about," he thought. "I'm going to experience what so many people felt before – so many of my heroes."

He thought of his favorite former Ohio State player, linebacker Chris Spielman.

"He wasn't the biggest linebacker, but he was relentless," Tank says. "Sideline to sideline, even 12, 20, 50 yards downfield he was running after you as hard as he possibly could.

"He played in 'The Game,' and I knew I was going to be part of 'The Game' and a Big Ten championship."

Again, he allowed himself to bask in that thought. He, Tank Whaley, was going to play an important role in an Ohio State-Michigan game, the winner of which would earn an outright Big Ten title and head to the Rose Bowl.

"Did I ever think I was ever going to be in a position like that? No," he said. "And am I? Yes. And in my mind, I was going to make every bit of it count."

The next morning, he stuck a camera in his pocket as he packed to head to the stadium. He had seen other players do this in the past, snap photos in a triumphant locker room. Good idea, he thought.

"This year, I'm going to play in it, and this is my last go-round," he thought, "and I want to remember it. I just had a good feeling about the game."

He should have had a good feeling that day as he walked into Michigan Stadium, aka "The Big House." Sunk below street level, without any decks, and with its unbroken roll of cascading seats, I think it looks more like "The Big Salad Bowl," but that's another story.

November 17 in Ann Arbor was cold, gray and rainy. A mist hung in the air. This was perfect weather for fullbacks. Tank was fired up.

"I was probably pretty dangerous," he says. "It's one of those times where they talk about you hitting a switch and you just want to kill somebody. I never had a chance to play in this rivalry, and I was finally involved."

For Whaley, the atmosphere probably took him back to his days of playing in Tanks Memorial Stadium, facing Portsmouth or Wheelersburg.

The only thing missing was mud. Michigan has artificial turf.

The footing was missing, too, early on. Boeckman and Beanie Wells both slipped, and the ball fell out of Boeckman's hands a few times, as well.

The big question for the Wolverines, who had rebounded from a disastrous 0-2 start, was the health of two of their stars, quarterback Chad Henne and running back Mike Hart. Henne had a separated shoulder and Hart a nagging ankle injury.

The Wolverines struck first, though, driving 49 yards in 11 plays and kicking a field goal late in the first quarter.

Whaley was in on just three plays in the first period. On two of them, he went out as an outlet receiver, and Boeckman was sacked both times.

In the second quarter, though, Beanie got untracked, and Whaley's playing time doubled to six plays. Coincidence?

Tank's lead block on linebacker Obi Ezeh helped Beanie convert a second-and-three with a 5-yard run.

Three plays later, the ball was at the Michigan 1-yard line, second and goal. Whaley lined up just wide of the tight end on the left and behind the line. He was supposed to come into motion back to the right and execute the lead block for Beanie, but

Boeckman, maybe rattled a bit, forgot to signal Whaley in motion and simply snapped the ball instead.

Whaley still managed to come slanting back to the right in time to smack Ezeh hard on the right shoulder, spinning him around and out of the play. Beanie then bulldozed straight through safety Brandent Englemon into the end zone for a touchdown and a 7-3 lead.

Two things stood out about that play. One was Whaley, celebrating with Beanie and teammates while standing over the fallen Englemon.

It gave Whaley a sense of déjà vu. Five years earlier, Whaley had sacked Englemon, then playing for Covington (Ky.) Holmes, and stood over him, celebrating.

The second thing was what ABC announcer Kirk Herbstreit said as they showed a replay. Herbstreit said, "Nice lead block by Bailey."

BAILEY??

Earlier in the game, Herbstreit's partner, Brent Musberger, had called Whaley "Wiley."

Whaley (42) blocks Michigan linebacker Max Pollock as Buckeyes tailback Beanie Wells (28) hits a hole. Whaley helped Wells rush for 222 yards in a 14-3 win on November 17, 2007 in Ann Arbor, Michigan (Photo by Jim Davidson)

"What the heck was that all about?" Whaley said later, after watching the tape of the game.

Boeckman threw an ill-advised pass just before halftime that gave Michigan a chance to retake the lead, but the OSU defense held and the 7-3 edge stood at the break.

On Ohio State's first play of the second half, Beanie broke to the left, executed a wicked juke that left Englemon grasping at air, and burst 62 yards for a TD.

Given his team's 14-3 lead, the weather, and Boeckman's recent shaky play, Tressel clearly decided to button down and hope Beanie and his defense were good enough to win this one.

Boeckman threw just two passes in the second half. But it mattered little, because Henne was just not himself. He consistently overthrew receivers, and when he was on target, star receiver Mario Manningham couldn't catch.

After some early success, Hart was finding nowhere to go, and Buckeyes defensive end Vern Gholston (three sacks) was beating right tackle Stephen Schilling like a rented mule.

As the game ground into the fourth quarter, Whaley was in his glory. He blocked Ezeh so often and so effectively the Michigan linebacker probably had Whaley's Buckeye-leaf helmet decals imprinted on his chest.

Tank sprung Beanie for a 23-yard run, then was on the field for 11 of Ohio State's 19 plays in the final period.

That included all eight plays of the game's final possession. It started on the Michigan 43 with 3:44 left. The Wolverines called time-outs after two OSU runs to bring up third-and-four.

Tank blasted linebacker Max Pollock off the edge of the left side, and Beanie picked up six yards and the first. Michigan stopped calling time-outs.

A few plays later, Whaley took great pleasure in driving Englemon the same way he drove Pollock, clear off the television screen.

Tank has never said this, but you wonder if somewhere, that Wittenberg recruiter who tried so hard to talk Whaley out of walking on at OSU was watching this game. If he was, he might have been squinting at the TV: "Is that? ...Naw, it can't be the same guy."

Whaley played a career-high 10 minutes that day. Beanie ended with 222 yards rushing, the most ever by a Buckeye against Michigan.

Tank kisses the Big Ten championship trophy immediately after the game in the Michigan Stadium locker room. (Family photo)

"That's a story I can keep forever and ever," Tank said. "I helped the cause that got Beanie Wells 220 yards in the Michigan game."

Running backs coach Dick Tressel called that day "Tank's finest hour."

His finest moment was about to come. On second down from the Michigan 5, the call came in: "Victory Formation."

That's the kneel-down. And that's when Tank Whaley allowed himself that moment of exultation, of throwing his arms skyward in the ultimate display of "We did it; I did it."

"I was satisfied with myself at that point," he said, and he wasn't talking only about that day. "There's no better feeling I'll probably experience in football than that time right there – the best rivalry in the sport, the best tradition, the biggest game.

"I grew up watching that game, and now I'm playing in it. I've been part of the program for five years, but now I've contributed. I beat them four times.

"There's so much stuff I feel part of now. I feel part of history. And it was just like, 'Wow.' I can hardly describe it. You want to hit your knees, but you don't. I just threw it up and looked, and everybody was running on the field and hugging. The celebration was on.

"I even ran over and jumped up on a chair and got into the fans for a little bit."

Afterward, the team gathered in the locker room. As they walked in, they were handed Big Ten championship hats.

Tressel spoke, emphasizing the magnitude of their achievement, winning back-to-back outright Big Ten titles. The Buckeyes assumed they were heading for the Rose Bowl for the first time in 23 years.

Then the Big Ten trophy appeared and was passed around. Whaley retrieved his camera and had teammates snap photos – hazy from the steam in the humid locker room – of him with the trophy.

"It was like, 'Wow, we've done something that people didn't think we were going to do,'" he said. "It's kind of like what I had to do my whole career. I had to always defy people, and then for this team to defy everyone and actually win it... at that moment, it was just like unbelievable. I couldn't express it. I was just on cloud nine."

CHAPTER 11:
Hometown Hero

The weeks following the Michigan game were like one long victory lap for Tank Whaley. He would be lauded and applauded, fawned over and sought after. It was as if five years of toiling in the parched desert were being rewarded with one huge, gully-washing downpour.

It did not take long after beating the Wolverines for Ohio State players and fans to realize that the notion of the Buckeyes playing for a national title wasn't as far-fetched as it once seemed.

A crazy college-football season was continuing to provide upset after shocking upset. The 2007 season was like watching the Berlin Wall fall, and then all the other satellite countries suddenly breaking away from the Soviet bloc. Upheaval was upon us.

In the same week as the Michigan game, losses by Oregon and Oklahoma propelled OSU up to fifth in the BCS standings, and two of the four teams ahead of the Buckeyes – Kansas and Missouri – had to play each other yet.

Suddenly, all OSU needed was two more upsets in the next two weeks. When Louisiana State lost to Arkansas on November 23, OSU was third.

That set up December 1, a dramatic evening of television viewing for the Buckeyes. If either No. 1 Missouri lost to Oklahoma, or No. 2 West Virginia lost to Pittsburgh, OSU was headed to New Orleans.

The majority of players gathered in the team meeting room that night, munched on pizza and watched together.

Oklahoma handled Missouri, which actually was the predicted outcome. That would have been enough to get the Buckeyes into the title game, but the bigger shock was unranked and downtrodden Pitt knocking off West Virginia.

When that game became a final, there was jubilation in the room.

"Everybody was going crazy," Whaley told the *Columbus* (Ohio) *Dispatch*. "Coach Tressel got a little smile on his face. He wasn't jumping around, he didn't show us his vertical leap, but I've been around him enough to know he was a happy man."

And just like that, OSU had risen from No. 7 to No. 1 – again.

Still buzzing from the evening's events, the Buckeyes had their annual awards banquet the next day. Held in an upscale hotel in downtown Columbus, it's quite a celebration. Families come to town, and players put on their suits and ties.

Whaley's Ironton clan made the two-and-a-half-hour trip, of course, and it proved well worth the drive.

Bo Rein was the type of player and person who was never satisfied, always striving to do more, to be better.

He was an Ohio State running back, a starter from 1964 to 1966, and played on OSU's 1966 national championship baseball team.

Former Buckeyes tight end Greg Lashutka was one of Rein's teammates.

"He was intense and passionate about life," Lashutka told the *Dispatch*. "You wanted him as a teammate. He was in the mold of that wonderful group of characters we had who pursued life real hard."

His dreams of playing professionally were cut short by injuries, and he turned to coaching, where he was equally driven and successful. In 1976, he became the nation's youngest college football coach at age 30 when he took over for Lou Holtz at William & Mary. Late in 1979, he was named to coach LSU.

He never strode the sidelines at a Tigers game, though. On January 10, 1980, he was returning from a recruiting trip in a small private plane when the cabin somehow suffered a loss of pressure.

The plane drifted over the Atlantic Ocean and crashed. No wreckage was found. Rein was dead at 34.

Ohio State honored its shooting-star former player by naming a postseason award after him. Each year, players vote for whom they consider to be the team's most inspirational player, and that player is given the Bo Rein Award.

Whaley was the clear-cut winner. He had earned his way into his teammates' hearts with his determination and his uphill fight for playing time.

In those early years, when he was Captain Scout Team, the offensive and defensive linemen were rooting for him to succeed. Then, when he switched positions early last season, the running backs got to know and like him. By the time December arrived, he was a popular guy in the locker room.

"That award fits him perfectly," quarterback Todd Boeckman said. "He's been through a lot – he's battled through so many just difficult situations out there, I have to give him a lot of credit. And he's got a great personality, he's funny, he's just a great guy."

Jim Tressel, too, did not hide his admiration for Tank.

Maybe part of that was because Tressel once was an under-sized (5-9) quarterback at a small college (Baldwin-Wallace). Maybe he once dreamed of walking on at a Division I school, as Tank had.

Maybe part of it was his appreciation for everything Whaley represented: a kid who wanted to be a Buckeye and did everything he possibly could to make it happen.

Tank with two big fans of his: Ohio State coach Jim Tressel (left) and Whaley's fiancée, Brittany Benjamin. (Family photo)

At any rate, Tressel made a point of approaching Tammy and Dave after the banquet and telling them how much Tank deserved the award.

More recently, Tressel eloquently summed up Whaley's contributions to the program.

"It meant so much to him to be part of the Ohio State family," Tressel says. "He was so appreciative and so excited that he had this opportunity and had these relationships; that he got to run out into the Horseshoe.

"To me, the fact that he found a way to contribute was just icing on the cake. Being a Buckeye for him was all he really ever wanted, and just because of his makeup, he found his way onto the field.

"It just goes to show there's a lot more to (the OSU football tradition) than Heisman Trophies or rings or All-Americans or draft choices. (Whaley) just brought something special. He added something to our group."

After learning LSU would be their opponent in the title game, the Buckeyes practiced for about three weeks, then had a week off for Christmas before heading to New Orleans.

Whaley returned to his hometown for a few days of relaxation – for the most part.

In recent years, Ironton has made some slow steps forward from the depressing days of shuttered mills and lost jobs.

The old Dayton Malleable/Ironton Iron plant at the corner of 3rd and Vine streets has been torn down. Symbolically, it's better to have a big open space in town rather than a hulking reminder of a lost era.

Town officials hope an investor sees the prime location as an opportunity.

Liebert Corporation and Emerson Electronics have come to the area recently, bringing several hundred new jobs.

There are plans now, and new beginnings. An annual Gus Macker basketball tournament draws in people. The riverfront is being studied – can an amphitheater be built there? The old railroad depot now houses several good restaurants.

Virginia Bryant, longtime resident and member of the Lawrence County Historical Society, says there is a new community spirit emerging.

"There are a lot of people taking an interest in volunteering, there's an excitement, we have plans now," Bryant said. "We're on the way back up, we're not giving in."

As Whaley's career began to take off at Ohio State, as it became clear he was going to make it after all, he started serving as an unwitting role model back home.

People put his pictures up on the walls of their stores or restaurant, pointed to them and said, "He's from here. He plays for Ohio State."

Dave Coburn, who helped train Tank in the summer of 2003, just before he reported to OSU, is one of those. He has several pictures on the wall of the physical-therapy center where he works.

"It's neat because it's a blue-collar town, and (Whaley) symbolizes hard work and what it takes to do something," Coburn said. "It's not always handed to you on a table. So many people here relate to him."

All the sudden, Whaley was a celebrity.

"One lady came in to pick up her cake and said, 'I remember diapering (Tank) when he was in daycare,'" Tammy says. "I'm like, 'Really?'"

She said little kids routinely would ride their bikes to her house, knock on the door and ask whether Tyler was there and if they could talk to him.

"No, honey, he's in Columbus," she would answer, but she might let them in to look at his pictures on the walls.

"Told you he lived here," one kid would say to his buddy on their way out.

Tammy would tell Tank about these encounters, and he just laughed it off.

If he didn't believe his fame in Ironton before, it would have been impossible to deny on that trip home he made before Christmas. Whaley was treated like the prodigal son returning.

He drove home on a Wednesday night and by Thursday, he had been asked to speak to three different groups of school kids. He accepted all three invitations.

With a highlight tape of LSU's defense in his front seat, he drove to Ironton Elementary, where Whaley had attended kindergarten through third grade.

As he walked in the front door, there was a stir. Soon people emerged from offices – secretaries and teachers who remember him walking these halls 12 or 15 years ago. There were hugs and whoops and smiles.

Marcus Williams was there, also. Williams is another Ironton High product who walked on at OSU – three years after Tank did – and saw some playing time at running back last season. On a few plays early last season, there was an all-Ironton backfield as Whaley blocked for Williams.

Dave and Brittany came with Tank. His grandparents, Tommy and Dotty Tipton, met him there, along with his cousin Brett, fully recovered from his November pacemaker surgery.

Also there was Tank's childhood friend Alexis Reedy, with her baby, who was wearing a "Poop on Michigan" T-shirt.

The gym was packed full of kids – the whole school. Charla Reedy, Alexis' mom and a school secretary, introduced Whaley and Williams to the gathered throng.

Reedy told the kids these were not only Ohio State football players, but "good boys."

She said the two were "living proof that if you put your mind to something, you can do it."

Williams and Whaley both spoke briefly and answered some questions. Then every kid was promised an autograph.

That was accomplished in a whirlwind tour of each classroom. They had only a few minutes before the end of the school day, so they were rushed up and down stairs and hallways, signing shirts, hats and scraps of paper at such a breakneck pace that Tank started sweating even though it was chilly outside.

As they left to more hugs and thank-yous, it was obvious that even though the two were relatively unknown players to most, in Ironton, they were larger than life.

Driving through town, Tank stopped at Tanks Memorial Stadium. He bumped into an old coach and friend there, Jeff Linn, who was one of the first to encourage him to walk on at OSU if that's what he really wanted.

The next stop was the home of his uncle Andy Whaley, who had recently finished redoing his basement to make it probably Ironton's ultimate Buckeye-watching spot. It featured a wood-paneled bar, refrigerator, and couches and chairs gathered around the television, with an Ohio Stadium mural painted on the wall behind the screen.

One entire glass-topped table contains nothing but articles about Whaley, from his high-school days to more recent accomplishments.

Tank then headed for his grandparents house, where dinner awaited. Tammy brought a birthday cake for Brittany, who was turning 22. It was decorated in Mardi Gras colors and style for the New Orleans trip they all would soon make.

Slowly Tammy is trying to cut back her workload. She's learning to say no once in awhile, particularly to last-minute wedding-cake requests when she's already swamped.

On this night, in his grandmother's kitchen, Tank Whaley was in his element. The room was warm and full of love and laughter. Stories were told, memories shared. Once again, he could be the entertainer that he is at heart.

Tank says he once assumed he would come back after college and settle down in Ironton – try to do his part to give back to the community.

"When I left, I always said I was going to go back where my whole family lived, and that's where I wanted to raise my family," he said. "My kids would play for the same high school I did."

Tank was treated like a rock star upon his return to Ironton for Christmas break in 2007. During a visit to his old elementary school, he autographs a shirt for Rachel Halterman. (Photo by Doral Chenoweth III for the Columbus (Ohio) Dispatch)

But meeting Brittany started to change those plans. They have decided to stick around Columbus and find jobs there. Being a former Ohio State football player is golden on the resume in central Ohio.

"I didn't experience a lot of things until I went to Ohio State," he said. "Then I got to go to Arizona and other places, which I never would have done if I never left Ironton. I think you need to experience the outside world. There's so much more out there."

Even while enjoying the brief respite from practice, though, Tank continued to work. Coburn said he showed up every day at 6 a.m. that week, working for an hour or two.

"He said he wanted to do all he could, that they had to beat LSU," Coburn says. "He didn't ever stop. He kept going."

Two weeks later in New Orleans, Whaley's family realized just how big Tank's story was becoming.

Walking around town with their "Whaley" jerseys on, the family was amazed to hear groups of Buckeyes fans – usually students – pass them and start chanting, "Tank, Tank, Tank!"

Tank's family basked in his success. Here they share a moment with Ohio State president E. Gordon Gee (middle). From left, they are his grandfather Tommy Tipton, grandmother Dotty Tipton, stepfather Dave Vogelsong and mother Tammy Vogelsong. (Family photo)

None of them had ever needed public recognition of Tank to feel he was validated or successful. Still, it was thrilling to know that people had noticed and were rooting for him now.

"We're not talking about a guy who played a lot," his grandfather Tommy Tipton said with a tone of amazement. "I mean, he's not Beanie. And yet everywhere we walked, people were coming up to us."

For the purposes of preserving the fairytale tone of this story, it would be best to skip over the national championship game. After the emotions at Michigan, the 38-24 loss to LSU was anticlimactic.

It probably suffices to say that unlike in 2006, Tank Whaley played in college football's biggest game of the season. It's also probably fair to say the best team won, that Ohio State overachieved in 2007.

Beanie Wells did break a 65-yard touchdown run against LSU, though, which helped him compile 1,609 rushing yards on the season. That was the highest total ever by an Ohio State sophomore – topping the 1,577 in 1974 by some guy named Archie Griffin.

As a team, the Buckeyes rushed for 196.9 yards a game last season, the most in the seven-year Jim Tressel era.

Both of those marks are something in which Whaley can legitimately stake a claim. He was an important part of that success, playing in all 13 games for a total of 69 minutes, more than he had played in 2005 and 2006 combined.

But Tank's story is much bigger than rushing yards or playing time or whether or not he earned a scholarship.

It's really about what can happen when someone sets his mind to something others told him was impossible. About not expecting or assuming anything, not getting discouraged even though there were a million moments where most of us would have been.

It's about using hard work and determination to squeeze every last drop out of your natural ability.

His stepfather, Dave, said there were times recently when he would read articles about Tank or hear Tressel mention him in an interview, that he would get goosebumps.

"You can't describe it," Dave says. "You stop and think that this is something so many kids really just dream about, that Tyler dreamed about. You couldn't have written this script five years ago and thought it would come true."

It's also about the satisfaction of earning everything he got. Of being happy with every small achievement, wanting more but at the same time not needing it to feel as if he had succeeded.

It's about finding your soul's reserve tank.

"Whatever he does, he gives you all he's got," Tommy Tipton says. "There's no three-quarters effort in him. He gives everything."

It's about representing a hard-luck town, giving the people you grew up with something to hold onto. About serving as an inspiration and an example for other undersized, big-hearted Ironton kids hoping to make it.

"The whole town has always been rooting for him," said his old weight-lifting coach, Larry Browning. "It's like a Cinderella story. You've heard of those before, but you didn't think you'd see it unfold right in front of you."

And at its core, Tyler Whaley's story is about a kid who dreamed of running out of the Ohio Stadium tunnel into that burst of light and noise and excitement, and who can look in the mirror today, tomorrow and 50 years from now and say, "I made it come true. I did it."

"I felt deep down inside that I could play Division I football," Tyler says. "I didn't want to live with regret saying I probably could have played, but I didn't do anything about it.

"So I basically just tell people to follow their dreams, work hard, and if it's right, doors will open and you'll be given an opportunity."

CHAPTER 12:
A New Dream

B y all rights, the story should end there, with the conclusion of Whaley's final season at Ohio State. We're talking about a kid who wasn't even recruited to play college ball, after all, so that logically should be the pinnacle.

Pro ball? Right. Even a year ago, if you had asked Tank Whaley if he thought he had an NFL future, you would have been treated to one of his hearty, life-is-good laughs.

Sure, Ohio State players attract NFL attention. The school gets dozens of pro scouts at its annual Pro Day workouts, so anyone who has played a role at all for the Buckeyes at least gets a chance to be seen.

But when the 2007 season ended, Whaley figured that was it for him.

Part of it was a cold-eyed, realistic view of his prospects. He had only one year of real highlights to show the scouts. He was a fullback, which is becoming as rare in the NFL as it is in college.

And he would be one of three Buckeyes fullbacks working out on Pro Day, joining Dionte Johnson and Trevor Robinson.

He wasn't sure he wanted to put himself through the two months of lifting and workouts and 40-yard dash practice it would take to get ready.

He talked to several agents, who gave it to him straight. There are three tiers of rookies entering the NFL each year. The top tier is draft picks, and Whaley knew he wouldn't be getting drafted. Only about five fullbacks get drafted each year, and one scouting service rated Whaley the 34th-best fullback available.

The next level is players who go undrafted, but whom teams call immediately after the draft and offer free-agent contracts. Each team usually signs somewhere between six and 15 such players. They are long shots, easily expendable.

But most years, one or two undrafted players make each NFL roster, so it's not a pipe dream.

The agents, though, told him he probably was in the lowest tier — a "camp guy" — lingo for a fringe prospect who might get invited to a minicamp to try out. They had a chance to be signed, but more likely, they would be given a quick bus or plane ticket home after a few practices.

So was it worth the work? Whaley asked Ohio State strength and conditioning coach Eric Lichter that one day in January.

"I said, 'I'm not going to put myself through all this. I might not even get a shot,'" Whaley said.

The other part of his thought process was that mentally, he felt he was ready to move on. He had accomplished all he had wanted in football. He was going to graduate in March. He was engaged.

Grounded as he is by his background and family, Tank felt like it was time to get a "real job."

"At the time, I had done some preliminary interviewing (with Columbus-area companies), and if I was going to seriously interview anywhere, I wanted to be able to accept a job offer and not say, 'Well, I'm going to try the NFL first,'" he said. "At the time, that seemed to have positives that outweighed trying out for the NFL."

His mother, Tammy, asked him what he was thinking, and Tank answered, "Mom, it would be a long shot for me. I need to be realistic, this is why I got my degree."

So he was just about to hang up the cleats when Lichter gave him some simple advice: Until you're faced with a decision, until you have a good job offer on the table and are forced to decide, why stop working out? You would be eliminating the football option. At least give it a shot on Pro Day.

Tank's fiancée, Brittany, agreed with Lichter's view.

"I told Tyler he'd really regret it if he didn't try it," she said. "You've proved yourself this far, you can do it again."

Whaley was convinced. And once he sets his mind to something, it's full go. So he settled into a routine of finishing up his final quarter of classes, working out, and trying to lose some more weight.

Along the way, the accolades kept coming.

In February, the National Football Foundation honored Tank and six other central Ohio collegians at its Scholar-Athlete awards banquet. Tammy and Dave came up, and Whaley wore a snazzy three-piece suit and posed for photos.

Not long after that, Whaley was one of four seniors to accompany Jim Tressel to the Ohio Statehouse, when the state Senate recognized the team's Big Ten title with Resolution No. 186.

The Buckeye contingent got two standing ovations and stuck around afterward to sign autographs.

Ohio State's Pro Day came March 7. In past years, when 10 or 15 Buckeyes stood to be drafted, the event drew scouts from all 32 NFL teams, plus several head coaches. Throngs of 50 to 75 were not uncommon.

This year, the Ohio State senior class was thinner, and the number of NFL people on hand reflected that. Still, one player working out was junior defensive end Vernon Gholston, who was giving up his final year at OSU and was projected as a top-10 pick.

So more than 20 NFL teams were represented, including one head coach (Marvin Lewis of the Cincinnati Bengals).

Tank was pleased with his performance. He did 34 repetitions of 225 pounds on the bench press, a few less than his best but still outstanding. He said he was clocked anywhere from the high 4.7-second to the low 4.9 range in the 40-yard dash, which put him at least in the general ballpark of other fullbacks entering the draft.

He weighed in at 252, at least 10 pounds lighter than he was during the season.

"I feel like I definitely helped myself," he said.

That performance gave him real hope he might get a chance somewhere. He was thrilled that several scouts and coaches spoke to him afterward. Maybe, maybe, football wasn't done with him yet.

On March 16, Tank Whaley graduated with a degree in health sciences. Before his final quarter, he had a 3.16 grade-point average.

After graduating, he lived a life of relative leisure for six weeks or so before the draft — no school, no job. All he had to do was work out a few hours each day.

Brittany was the breadwinner through that time. She was interning at a chain of funeral homes in the Columbus area, and she laughed at their different schedules.

"I have to get up at 5:30 or 6:00 to go to work, and I'll ask him to text me when he gets up," she said. "And then I had to ask him to text me at 8:00 whether he was up for the day or not, because I didn't want to know if he's sleeping any later than that."

The draft was the weekend of April 26-27. The first two rounds were held Saturday and the final five on Sunday. That's when Tank figured he might get a call as soon as the draft ended.

He spent the weekend in Ironton. On Sunday, he was at Tammy's house, getting ready to head over to his grandmother's place for a meal.

At 11 a.m., just an hour after the draft had resumed, he got a call. It was the Bengals running backs coach.

As soon as Tammy realized Tank was talking to an NFL team, she started screaming. She can't help it.

"He had to run outside, because he couldn't hear the coach," Tammy says. "I followed him outside, and he was holding his hand down, like, 'Stop?'"

He wasn't getting drafted, but the Bengals wanted him to know they were interested. If he didn't get drafted, they were putting in an early word that they'd like to call him back and sign him to a free-agent deal.

The reason for Tammy's screaming wasn't just that an NFL team had called her son, it was that the Bengals had called.

This is the team young Tyler had grown up following. It's a natural for Ironton kids, since the high school's mascot is the Tigers, and the colors are the same as the Bengals: orange and black.

"For the longest time, he had Bengals wallpaper up in his room," Tammy says. "We had pictures of him dressed in full Bengals gear."

Sure enough, the moment the draft ended, the Bengals called Whaley back. They were offering a two-year deal (non-guaranteed, so the length is mostly irrelevant) and a $3,000 signing bonus. He can keep the three grand no matter what happens — even if he had been cut the next day — so that's not irrelevant.

Tank spoke to his agent and told him to take the deal. Later, the Kansas City Chiefs also called, but Whaley hadn't expected other teams to be interested and he'd already taken the Cincinnati deal.

Why wait, anyway? This was the chance he thought he couldn't get. Yet again, doors were opening in front of him.

"It's another dream come true," he said. "I didn't ever think I'd be walking on at Ohio State, it was crazy to get that shot — and then to go to the team I grew up watching.

"I couldn't ask for more."

That was Sunday. On Thursday, he was due to report to Cincinnati for the start of a three-day minicamp just for rookies.

Life changes in a hurry. And it didn't take long for him to realize the differences between college and pro ball.

At Ohio State, he felt pressure when he arrived as an undersized walk-on in 2003, certainly. But there's a different vibe around a college program – even as an obscure walk-on, Whaley wasn't in danger of being released.

At worst, he would be allowed to practice all season and dress for home games. That's not a bad deal, even if it never got any better than that.

In the NFL, one bad play in rookie minicamp — one bonehead mistake — and the Bengals could decide Whaley had no chance to stick, and they could send him home.

"The difference is in college, you might have a sense that you might not belong, but you know you have time to pick it up," Whaley said. "In the NFL, you could be really good, but in three months, it's 'See you later.' It's a little bit different, you're fighting for survival. At Ohio State, I don't want to say there was a comfort level, but you weren't going anywhere."

On Thursday, May 1, he reported to minicamp, got a physical, got an offensive playbook, a special teams playbook, and then an introductory talk from the coaches about what to expect for the next three days.

On Friday morning, the fun began. There were two practices a day for the next two days.

"If we weren't in practice, we were in meetings," Whaley said. "You had about 15 or 20 minutes to shovel some food down, and then you were already back in a meeting. It was like boot camp, like a military schedule. It's hard to sit down.

"After the first practice, I cut the tape off, took a shower, and went right back in to get my ankles retaped."

He was overwhelmed at first.

"It's a whole new level of competition, and you know you're with elite guys," he said.

And he noticed an immediate difference in the tone. Finally he was realizing what all those former college players say when they turn pro – that college football is the best time of their lives, don't be in a hurry to leave. Pro ball a business, and there is not the camaraderie and "school spirit" that exists at a place like Ohio State.

"These coaches are different," he said. "I'm used to Doc (Ohio State running backs coach Dick Tressel) and Coach Tressel. They're laid back. They expect you to get it done, and if you mess up, they tell you what you did wrong and you better get it right next time.

"You walk in to Cincinnati, and these coaches have a whole new expectation. Their heads are on the line. At Ohio State, the program is usually up there, but the Bengals are trying to push over the top of the hill, and the coaches are feeling pressure wanting to turn the organization around.

"You mess up one play, they're in your face yelling, and you're like, 'Dang.' But that's part of the sport. If your feelings get hurt, you don't belong."

Meanwhile, Whaley was a bit star-struck. Quarterback Carson Palmer attended the first day of minicamp. Even though Whaley didn't get to personally speak with him, he said he felt the same way he did when he arrived at Ohio State in the summer of 2003.

"At the time, they were coming off the national championship season, which I had watched on television," Whaley said. "So I was like, 'Oh my gosh, there's (quarterback) Craig Krenzel, there's (running back) Maurice Clarett.'

"I was like that here. Carson clearly is the leader and the heart and soul of the team, and even though he didn't have to be here (for rookie minicamp), I think he just wanted to make his presence known."

Whaley said Friday and Saturday's practices were tough, but he started feeling better by the Sunday morning session, the last of the weekend.

"I started getting the hang of what to do," he said. "I started picking up the plays and I felt comfortable. I felt I left on a good note."

Whaley's battle is uphill, but not impossibly steep.

The Bengals have a veteran fullback, Jeremi Johnson, who has been a steady and solid contributor since being drafted in the fourth round in 2003. And they signed Whaley and another undrafted free agent, Bradley Glathhaar of the University of Cincinnati, to provide competition for Johnson in camp.

There's a chance that even if Whaley or Glathhaar don't make the 53-man roster, one could be kept on the practice squad. Those players earn a decent weekly check and practice with the team all week, sort of like a scout-teamer in college.

They can be activated at any time.

As this book went to press, Whaley was getting ready to return to Cincinnati for the start of offseason workouts. Another minicamp would be held in June. Every day he's on the roster is a good day, really.

"I know I can be gone in a heartbeat, so it's going to be a matter of getting to training camp (which opened in late July), putting on full pads, hitting people and showing them what they want to see," Whaley said. "I hope I can be part of the 53. I take it as I did at Ohio State, I know I'm starting at the bottom, and the question is, am I going to be in the NFL and making money?"

It's the same, but then it's not the same, either. This should not be taken to mean playing in the NFL isn't important to Tank Whaley, because now that he's got a shot, he's as driven as ever.

But the difference is that when he came to Ohio State, he knew deep down he was good enough to make it there. He was filled with a burning passion to prove all the doubters and recruiters wrong.

With pro ball, he's not positive he's good enough. He's going to find out by giving it his best shot, but he won't be crushed if he gets released.

"I'm still chasing a dream, and in my mind, I'll do whatever it takes to accomplish that dream," he said. "But like, I wouldn't accept failure at Ohio State. I was just going to keep pushing and pushing until somebody let me play.

"But with the NFL, I'm going to give my best and go the hardest I can go. And if that's not good enough, that's OK. It's not a do-or-die thing like Ohio State."

He's got a life, is what he's saying. With his slim prospects heading into draft weekend, he had a backup plan. Whaley had been interviewing for sales jobs in the Columbus area, and he's confident he'll have little trouble finding a position if the NFL doesn't work out.

Then of course, there is the wedding on December 6 to plan. That date might have to be changed if he sticks in the NFL — which would qualify as a good problem to have.

So no matter what happens with the Bengals, he already has accomplished more than he was ever expected to accomplish. The NFL call was gravy.

"If I get cut, I'll say, 'Thanks for the opportunity,'" Whaley said. "That's all I ever wanted. I'll come back to Columbus and get a job and work and be a family man. I'm not one of those people who needs another team to pick me up, I've made up my mind that I'm not going to fly around the country looking for another chance. The Bengals are my shot.

"If I can play, I'll ride that ride as long as I can. I'll work my butt off until the ride ends. If that's two months, or three or four years, once it ends, I'm ready for life after football."

And already, after just 23 years, what a life it has been.

Afterword

by Tyler Whaley

I have been very blessed with the opportunities I have been given. Even though opportunities presented themselves, it was always up to me to go after them with all I had.

There were hard times, but fighting through those times gave me satisfaction when overcoming them. I always wanted to be someone, so I was willing to do whatever it took to achieve that.

Even though I have achieved a lot, I will never slow down in doing whatever necessary to do the things I want to do.

I will forever be a son of Ironton, Ohio, and I am very proud of that. I always wanted to make sure I was giving Ironton a good name. I wanted to make the community that I'm from proud to say, "That boy is from here."

I will also always be grateful for the community of Columbus, Ohio, because they took me in and allowed me to experience the best times of my life. The city of Columbus is great, the people and community are great, and the tradition is unbelievable. I am proud to say I am truly a Buckeye.

I know I could not have reached these places in my life if not for my family and the communities of Ironton and Columbus. With all of that support, it gave me a driving force and determination to make it. It gave me power and a mindset of doing whatever it took to get where I wanted to be.

My family gave me the internal structure and toughness that I turned to many times throughout my life. It helped me overcome obstacles and adversity that stood in my way.

The community of Ironton always gave me support, from growing up as a Fighting Tiger to becoming an Ohio State Buckeye. Knowing I have the whole community, where I have spent the majority of my life, behind me was a fire that drove me to have the motivation to succeed for everyone in that town.

The community of Columbus took me in and allowed me to learn how to become a man. It allowed me to experience things I would never be able to experience anywhere else. I have been blessed to receive the best education and play the best football that a young man could play.

Growing up, I could only dream about being where I am now. You can say that I am living my dream. I regret not one thing in my life so far.

I feel I have earned where I am at and that makes everything I am fortunate to receive that much better. I have run "physical fitness" in the dusty fields to earn the orange and black, and I have played every snap of scout team for years to earn the scarlet and gray.

I was willing to do whatever was asked of me and more to achieve my goals. I always wanted to be the best, but I was not the best at times. That is what motivated me to work as hard as I could so I could compete and prove myself.

As I proved myself, opportunities presented themselves, too. I truly believe that it came from my willingness to do anything it took and my work ethic.

Coach Tressel talked about a book called *Talent is Never Enough*, by John Maxwell, which we as a team studied before the 2007 football season.

It was a book that truly hit home, because I was a boy that supposedly did not have talent like other Division I athletes, but I was ready to do the things that did not take talent that would allow me to compete with kids that were supposed to blow me away.

It was a great book, and I saw myself being the person the book was describing.

If I could leave a lesson from my life it would be to always chase your dreams. I was a kid who dreamed big and was willing not to just dream but to chase my dream through hard work and determination.

I was never scared of failing, because I did not want that to hold me back. If I was scared of failing, I would have never gone to Ohio State, where people told me I did not belong.

I used all the negatives for motivation and strived to be the best I could. I would tell people that you do not always have to be the most talented or recognized, but you just have to be the one who will work the hardest and do all that is necessary to get the job done.

I would also like to just say thanks. Thanks to the communities of Ironton and Columbus for all their support. It got me through tough times to know I had everyone behind me pushing me to be my best.

I would like to give a big thanks to my family back in Ironton. You all were truly my inspiration and taught me the true values of life that I will always carry with me. I also want to thank the newest member of my family, Brittany, for being with me and always encouraging me.

Finally, I want to say thank you to everyone for being with me on the best ride of my life. Having people around whom you love gives you that burning desire to be the best person you can be, not for just yourself but for them.

Thank you to everyone for all your support.

Acknowledgments

I've never liked that "last but not least" thing, I've always preferred "first things first."

So I have to start by saying that I am a humble servant of God. Anything I achieve in this life is simply a reflection of His glory, and that of His son, Jesus Christ.

Among earthly beings, I would not be who I am without the love and support of my wife, Faith, my stepson, Michael, and my daughter, Lindsey. I thank them for their patience and for picking up my slack around the house as I sweated over the keyboard and generally stressed out these past few months. I love you guys with all my heart.

My parents have always been a source of love and support, which I don't take for granted.

I want to thank the people at Cardinal Publishers Group, and in particular Tom Doherty, for taking a chance on a first-time author and an idea that may have seemed a bit of a stretch at first. I hope this was worth their while.

Tyler Whaley has been wonderful throughout the process. You are first-class, my man.

Likewise, Tyler's family was amazing to me from the first time I met them. They graciously put up with repeated phone calls to check names, dates and facts. They turned over treasured family photos. They laughed with me — and maybe at me!

Thank you Tammy, Dave, Tommy, Dotty, Missy, Andy and Rich, just to name those with whom I had the most contact. Tammy, those baked goods absolutely are the best I've ever tasted!

I am indebted to Virginia Bryant and the Lawrence County Historical Society for the photos and information. Thanks to Brittany Benjamin for giving me the inside scoop on her fiancée.

I appreciate football coaches Jim Tressel and Mark Snyder taking a few minutes out of their packed schedules to grant interviews, and in Mark's case, for writing the foreword.

Thanks also to Jim Ridgeway, Tom Low, Billy Bruce, Scott Terna, Jim Davidson, Steve Davis and the *Columbus Dispatch* for their photos. We didn't use them all, but I am grateful for everyone's willingness to help.

Finally, I thank fellow authors Austin Murphy, Bob Hunter and Jeff Snook for their advice and encouragement as I took what for me was a rather scary leap. I hope I land safely.

– Ken Gordon, April 7, 2008